# SHE OFFERED THEM CHRIST

*The Legacy*
*of Women Preachers*
*in Early Methodism*

## PAUL W. CHILCOTE

*Abingdon Press*
NASHVILLE

SHE OFFERED THEM CHRIST:
THE LEGACY OF WOMEN PREACHERS IN EARLY METHODISM

*Copyright © 1993 by Abingdon Press*

*This book is printed on recycled, acid-free paper.*

**Library of Congress Cataloging-in-Publication Data**

Chilcote, Paul Wesley, 1954-
  She offered them Christ : the legacy of women preachers in early Methodism/ Paul W. Chilcote.
      p.      cm.
  Includes bibliographical references and index.
  **ISBN 0-687-38345-5 (alk. paper)**
      1. Women, Methodist—England—History—18th century.   2. Women clergy—England—History—18th century.   3. Wesley, John, 1703-1791—Influence.   4. Methodist Church—England—History—18th century.   5. England—Church history—18th century.   6. Preaching—England—History—18th century.   I. Title.
BX8345.7.C46      1993
287'.082—dc20
                                                                92-31400
                                                                CIP

Scripture marked GNB are from the *Good News Bible*—Old Testament: Copyright © American Bible Society 1976; New Testament: Copyright © American Bible Society 1966, 1971, 1976. Used by permission.

95 96 97 98 99 00 01 02 03 04 — 10 9 8 7 6 5 4 3

MANUFACTURED IN THE UNITED STATES OF AMERICA

*To*
*all women who have*
*offered Christ in word and deed*
*for the life*
*of the world;*
*but especially for*
*Janet, my wife,*
*and my daughters,*
*Sandy, Rebekah, Anna, and Mary*

# *Contents*

# Introduction

Women helped to make the Wesleyan revival in England a powerful religious awakening. Their search for truth and justice brought vitality to the movement. The early Methodists not only rediscovered lost truths for the community of faith, but their faith also led them to confront the injustices of their world. Methodist women dared to claim their rightful place within the life of the church. They challenged repressive institutions. They questioned the validity of exclusive structures. The women preachers stood on the cutting edge of this struggle for liberation.

Through the generations, women have participated in this amazing Methodist tradition of witness and service. The painful struggle for acceptance and recognition, however, continues to this day. Consider, for example, Elizabeth Bautista. Her story, like the story of most Methodist women, is rooted deeply in the Christian faith. Administrator of three schools and pioneer founder of a medical clinic for impoverished villagers, Elizabeth also preaches three Sundays a month in a refurbished United Methodist church.

"The bishop recognizes my church work," she explains. "I have sought to be ordained to serve the country people, but there are very few ordained women in the Philippines. Even though I have been a deaconess for fifteen years and in charge of the two churches, they say to me each year, 'maybe next year.'"

Elizabeth's story is typical. It is repeated in the lives of women many times over. Whenever I have shared some of my knowledge about the early Methodist women preachers with female colleagues, the response has always been the same. "If only I had known about these women!" "If only the people of my church could be made aware of this rich legacy within our own tradition!" For those who are now serving parishes that have never before experienced women as pastors, the discovery of this lost family history could open minds and soften hearts. It might even open a few doors. It will certainly enrich the ministry of all.

In the chapters that follow, you will encounter the lives of some exceptional women. They were exceptional, not because they possessed extraordinary gifts, but because they allowed God to use fully whatever they had. God takes that which is ordinary, you see, and invests it with eternal significance and sacred power when it is offered freely for others. These women had the courage to offer Christ to their world. It was a world, not unlike our own, that generally preferred darkness to light. When these women caught a vision of God's dream for their lives and their world, however, nothing could stand in their way. They pursued that dream to its end.

The story of the women preachers, therefore, is one of realized potential—of maturity in Christ. It is inspiring because it elicits the best in all of us, male and female alike. For this very reason, the recovery of this legacy can help each of us to be more fully human. Enter into this study, then, with a great sense of appreciation. Expect to be changed in the process of discovery. May this study both enlarge your understanding and deepen your faith. That is my greatest hope for you.

Do not conform yourselves to the standards of this world, but let God transform you inwardly by a complete change of your mind.

Romans 12:2 GNB

Paul Wesley Chilcote

# Chapter 1

 *A Process
of Liberation
Begins*

## Roots of English "Female Preaching"

The lives of women often provide the most faithful models of Christian discipleship. Ever since the day of the Resurrection, women have proclaimed the good news they discovered in Christ. So the women preachers of early Methodism hardly represented something new in the life of the Christian community. Rather, they were a unique manifestation of a recurring theme. The prominence of women is conspicuous in every era of revival in the history of the church. Riding the crest of waves of renewal, women have boldly affirmed the liberating message of equality in Christ.

As early as the seventh century, women held prominent positions in the infant church in the British Isles. St. Hilda, abbess of Whitby, founded a monastic community for both men and women in A.D. 659. Known affectionately as "Mother," she provided important leadership in a critical period of the church's life. In the late Middle Ages, Lollard women were noted for their zealous preaching throughout the countryside. Renewal within the church in the sixteenth century brought women to the fore once again. Even Luther, the great German reformer, conceded that under some exceptional circumstances, it would be necessary for women to preach.

When reform came to the English Church certain exceptional women were undaunted in their proclamation of the gospel. The opposition was strong. It was even risky simply to defend the principles of their cause. When John Lambert advocated such innovations in 1538, for instance, he was promptly burned at the stake. So in spite of numerous exceptions, the general rule of the church remained and was inflexibly applied: "Her part is to hold her tongue, to learn in silence."

It was not until the boisterous seventeenth century that the practice of female preaching really took hold. The rise of English Puritanism fired the explosion. The Puritan movement, like the reforming tradition that preceded it and the evangelical revival that followed it, stressed the spirit of primitive Christianity, the simplicity of worship, and the sacredness of the individual before God. Some of the more radical expressions of this ethos, such as the Anabaptists, Brownists, Familists, Levellers, and Quakers, pushed the notions of spiritual equality, freedom of thought, and right of conscience to their logical conclusions.

One of the common practices that emerged during this period was known as "prophesying." Probably originating in the Puritan stronghold of Northampton, this activity included biblical exposition, testimony concerning Christian experience, and exhortation of the faithful, all of which generally followed the normal preaching. John Robinson, pastor of the Pilgrims, defined this practice in 1625. Demonstrating the equality of those called to this office, he wrote:

> Into the fellowship of this work are to be admitted not only the ministers, but the teachers too, as also the elders and deacons, yea, even of the multitude *(ex ipsa plebe)*, which are willing to confer their gift received of God, to the common utility of the church.[1]

It was but a small step from "any person" exercising the gift of prophecy in a service of worship to that same person entering the pulpit to preach in the more formal sense. And if unordained men were allowed to preach, the next logical step would be the prophesying and then the preaching of women as well. Some women took that step without hesitation.

When Arthur Lake, bishop of Bath and Wells, discovered one of the "she-preachers" in his own diocese, he unleashed the fury of his venomous wrath upon his errant flock:

> Certainly you have . . . showed yourselves unworthy to be men, that could be so weak as to become scholars to a woman; I cannot tell how better to resemble your humor, than to the distemperate appetite of girls that have the green-sickness, their parents provide for them wholesome food, and they get into a corner and eat chalk, and coals, and such like trash. So you that may in the Church have grave and sound instructions for the comfort of your souls, in Conventicles feed upon the raw, and undigested meditations of an ignorant usurping Prophetess.[2]

By mid-century, women preachers could be found in almost every part of the country, in cities and villages alike. Mrs. Attaway, famous for her exploits in London, preached weekly at the General Baptist Church in Bell Alley. It was not unusual for her to draw a crowd of several hundred seekers who stood attentive to her every word. The thought of spontaneous congregations gathering around such women infuriated John Vickers. He lashed out in a typical pamphlet of the day:

> Bold impudent housewives, without all womanly modesty . . . take upon them (in the natural volubility of their tongues, and quick wits or strong memories only) to prate (not preach or prophesy) . . . and that most directly contrary to the Apostle's inhibitions.[3]

In contrast to this common response, there were voices that spoke out in defense of women's preaching and the place of women in the church in general. Samuel Torshell, for instance, maintained that there was no difference between men and women in the state of grace. In the treatise of 1645, *The Womans Glorie,* he defended a radically egalitarian view of the true Christian community. Likewise, John Rogers wrote forcefully about the rights of women in the church and encouraged his female colleagues in their pioneering work: "Hold fast your liberty; keep your ground which Christ hath got and won for you, maintain your rights, defend your liberties even to the life; lose it not, but be courageous and keep it."[4]

The Society of Friends, or Quakers, seemed to make the greatest amount of progress toward sexual equality within the life of their community. Since all Christians possess the Light of Christ within and are illumined by the Holy Spirit, George Fox (founder of the Society) would say, no one should be disqualified from speaking as the Spirit gives him or her utterance. A former Baptist, Elizabeth Hooten, became his "first publisher of the truth" in 1648. She suffered imprisonment four times in England and endured the indignities of the barbarous Cart and Whip Act of 1661 when she proclaimed her faith in Boston.

Margaret Fell, her co-worker and later wife of the founding father, wrote one of the most persuasive defenses for women's preaching in a small tract entitled *Womens Speaking Justified* (1666). This classic treatise, described by many as the "pioneer manifesto of women's liberation," not only defends the right of women to speak as God's instruments, but also advocates their full participation in every aspect of religious life. There is no question that this "mother of Quakerism" did more than any single individual to guide and shape the lives of many aspiring women in her day and beyond.

While the ministry of women was developed within the Society of Friends to an unprecedented degree, Fox and his followers were simply irrigating a channel already made. Women, at least for a brief span of time, were able to realize their equal partnership with men. The phenomenon of women's preaching in the Wesleyan revival of the following century exhibits strikingly similar characteristics. In the evangelical revival under the Wesleys, the waters of reform and renewal would once again sweep through the ever-widening channel of human equality, women riding the crest of the wave.

## Eighteenth-century Backdrop

The early eighteenth century has often been called an age of conservatism. In retrospect, the previous century must have appeared a strange, violent, fanatical world. Having weathered the tremendous social upheavals during its civil war period, England seemed to be entering a new age of security.

At the same time, however, life in Britain and throughout Europe was in a state of transition. No aspect of English life would remain untouched by the momentous events that rocked all of Western culture at the dawn of the "modern era." Herbert Butterfield captured the spirit of the times:

> One of the vivid impressions left by the history of eighteenth-century England is that of broadening sweep and gathering momentum. It is as though a wave, moving only slowly at first—lightly combing the face of the water—collected from the sea increasing power, and finally arched itself into a thunderous mass.[5]

One of the most vital aspects of this society in transition was the increasing importance placed upon the position of women. To be sure, many forces were at work to keep women "in her place." Pamphlets such as *A Discourse of women, shewing their imperfections alphabetically* (translated from the French at the turn of the century), attempted to perpetuate the dehumanizing attitudes of the past. But critics of these traditional ideals and caricatures of womanhood were attracting larger audiences. Those committed to feminist reform, from Daniel Defoe to Lady Montagu, could not be silenced.

Many women founded their hope for liberation in education. Mary Astell, considered by most to be the first English feminist, described new vistas opening to women through education in her *Serious Proposals to the Ladies.* When Mary Wollstonecraft addressed the issue of women's political involvement in her famous *Vindication of the Rights of Women,* the earth was shaken by the debate that ensued. The social, political, and industrial revolutions of the late eighteenth century all reflect the increasing turbulence of an age in the process of transformation.

Another powerful agent of change in England was the religious revival, generally known as "evangelicalism." This spark of renewal ignited a flame that swiftly spread through the arid and listless churches of the land. The church had suffered greatly from the turmoil of the seventeenth century. It was in a state of decay. In response to the religious fanaticism of the previous century, which had torn the nation in two, church leaders denounced all forms of religious "enthusiasm." Dryden captured the pervasive fear of civil anarchy rooted in religious fervor in his famous lines from "Absalom and Achitophel":

> A numerous Host of dreaming saints succeed;
> Of the true old enthusiastic breed:
> 'Gainst form and order they their power employ
> Nothing to build and all things to destroy.

The Wesleyan revival shook the nation out of the religious paralysis created by that fear.

One of the consequences of the state of affairs prior to the revival, however, was the virtual disappearance of women preachers. Even within the Society of Friends there was marked decline in the activity of women at all levels. May Drummond was, perhaps, the one great exception to the dearth of women preachers in the early 1700s. Thousands of people flocked to hear this fluent speaker preach. She was indeed a shining light in a dark and cheerless morn, and even poets sang her praise:

> No more, O *Spain!* thy Saint *Teresa* boast;
> Here's one outshines her on the *British* coast,
> Whose soul like hers views one Almighty end,
> And to that centre all its motions tend,
> Too long indeed our sex, has been deny'd,
> And ridicul'd by men's malignant pride.[6]

There were also some shadowy figures who emerged from time to time, often doing more harm than good for the cause of women. Throughout the course of the century several exotic Spiritualist groups developed small, but highly visible, followings. The experience of "prophetesses" in these groups—charismatic visionaries and spiritual mediums—stunned and often frightened their contemporaries. While these mystery cults seldom identified with the Christian community, they contributed greatly to the prejudice of many against the public ministry of women.

In 1706, for instance, a large group of French immigrants fleeing persecution in Europe arrived in England. "French prophetesses" such as Betty Gray and "Pudding Pie Moll" aroused the fury of the London mob with their naked, violent orations and immoral conduct. Similar visionary strains within the Christian community were manifest in groups such as the Philadelphians, Shakers, and Millenarians, all of which were founded by women. Led by Mrs. Leade, "Mother Jane" Wardley, Ann Lee, and Joanna Southcott, these groups soon became an embarrassment to the Society of Friends out of which they emerged. Not even the Quakers, generally noted for their spirit of toleration, were willing to countenance such excesses.

## Wesley and Women

Nothing could have been further from this world of ecstatic prophetesses than the restrained, ordered, methodical world of the Epworth rectory. And yet, here, in the disciplined environment of his home, John Wesley received his first lesson about human equality. His primary teacher and example? Susanna, his mother.

It is difficult to exaggerate the influence that Susanna Wesley exerted on her sons and consequently upon the religious revival they helped to ignite. A daughter of the Puritan movement, Susanna was schooled by her father in the solid piety that had brought him to prominence as the "St. Paul of Nonconformity." She drank deeply from the wells of English Puritanism and carried its revolutionary spirit into her own home. In her simple style of life, her devotion to spiritual disciplines, and her sensitivity to the theological issues of her day, she had few peers.

It was her role as "pastor," however, that bears so directly upon this study, for Susanna was the major precursor of the early Methodist women preachers. At the time of her death, Wesley observed that "even she (as well as her father and grandfather, her husband, and her three sons) had been, in her measure and degree, a preacher of righteousness."[7] She was by all accounts the priestess of her family, but also minister to the Epworth parish as well. Her activities not only shaped Wesley's understanding of the Christian faith, they also reinforced his views concerning the rightful place of women in the life of the church.

Susanna followed in the footsteps of many women preachers of the previous century. Above all else in the Christian life she valued the sanctity of the inner conscience and the present activity of the Holy Spirit. These were emphases she retained from her Puritan heritage in spite of her teen-age conversion to the Church of England.

In 1702 she boldly proclaimed her Protestant manifesto in a letter to a friend: "I value neither reputation, friends, or anything, in comparison of the simple satisfaction of preserving a conscience void of offence towards God and man."[8]

When Samuel Wesley, her husband and rector of St. Andrew's Church in Epworth, was called away to Parliament in London during the winter months of 1710–1712, Susanna took his responsibilities for spiritual nurture and care upon herself. "I cannot but look upon every soul you leave under my care," she advised Samuel in 1712, "as a talent committed to me under a trust by the great Lord of all the families."[9]

Shortly thereafter, the demands of her conscience led to a startling discovery:

> At last it came into my mind, though I am not a man, nor a minister of the gospel, and so cannot be engaged in such a worthy employment as they were, yet . . . I might do somewhat more than I do. . . . I might pray more for *the people,* and speak with more warmth to those with whom I have an opportunity of conversing. However, I resolved to begin with my own children.[10]

Evening prayers that she conducted for her family quickly took the form of religious services. When townspeople flocked to the rectory to participate in her devotional exercises, she continued to expand the services of "public worship" despite possible repercussions. An inept curate whom Samuel had left in charge criticized Susanna for usurping the authority of her husband. He fired off a letter to Samuel in London. And when the rector requested his wife to explain her actions, Susanna's response was swift and clear.

She observed that while the curate's services attracted no more than twenty or twenty-five persons, her gatherings could boast between two or three hundred. Moreover, her labors produced specific fruit. Relationships among the townspeople improved. People were excited about their faith and desired to know more about God. She agreed with Samuel concerning the impropriety of a woman taking the lead in such matters. But she believed that the life of the church hung in the balance and no other course of action was left open to her.

The strength of her convictions and the justification of her pastoral vocation were set forth in no uncertain terms in a final word to the rector:

> If you do, after all, think fit to dissolve this assembly, do not tell me that you desire me to do it, for that will not satisfy my conscience: but send me your *positive command,* in such full and express terms as may absolve me from all guilt and punishment for neglecting this opportunity of doing good when you and I shall appear before the great and awful tribunal of our Lord Jesus Christ.[11]

Samuel wisely backed off. The highly successful ministry of his wife continued to renew the religious life of that early "society" within the church.

A special bond had always existed between John and his courageous mother. The well-known rectory fire of 1709 and "little Jackie's" miraculous escape reinforced that unique relationship. Susanna's formation of a "religious society" in her home and her pastoral activities within the community must have exerted a tremendous influence upon her impressionable son. She planted the seeds that later matured into Wesley's own Methodist Societies and his slow, but eventual, acceptance of women preachers. Susanna handed down a legacy of faith to her son in which one conviction remained primary. No one, not even a woman, ought to be prohibited from doing God's work in obedience to the inner calling of her conscience. Wesley never forgot.

It was inevitable that the "femininity of his early environment," as V. H. H. Green has called it, would have abiding consequences in Wesley's life.[12] A perceptive contemporary observed the way in which Wesley was particularly drawn to women:

> It is certain that Mr. Wesley had a predilection for the female character; partly, because he had a mind ever alive to amiability, and partly from his generally finding in females a quicker and fuller responsiveness to his own ideas of interior piety and affectionate devotion.[13]

It is unfortunate that the mention of John Wesley and women so often conjures up images of a succession of abortive relationships: a bungled romance in Georgia, a tragic engagement with Grace Murray, a disastrous marriage to a psychotic widow. On the contrary, Wesley's relationships with women were both extensive and rewarding.

Women continued to figure prominently in Wesley's life once he left the bounds of his parental home. Sally Kirkham, his "religious friend" of Oxford days, functioned as a spiritual adviser and guide. She led him to important devotional resources that shaped the course of his life. As a missionary in Georgia, Wesley experimented in the use of women in the life of the church. In an attempt to recapture the spirit of the early church, he appointed "deaconesses" to teach, to visit the sick, and to minister to the spiritual needs of his unwieldy parish.[14]

Wesley's encounter with the Moravians, a devout group of Lutheran Pietists from Germany, confirmed his own efforts. Their women leaders were divided into various orders such as nurses, widows, deaconesses, and eldresses. The "chief eldress" oversaw the work of the women and was often in a position of great power and influence. Wesley learned more about the functions of these women during a subsequent pilgrimage to Herrnhut in Germany, the primary center of Moravian influence.

In 1738–1739, when Wesley began to organize "united societies" within the Church of England for the renewal of "primitive Christianity," women were essential to the life of these small groups. When Elizabeth Fox, a leader in the Oxford Society, was anticipating a move, Wesley wrote her an impassioned letter to dissuade her leaving. In an appended note to her husband, he wrote: "The reason against her going hence is as evident as it is weighty: we have no one here like-minded . . . nor could the enemy devise so likely a means of destroying the work which is just beginning among them as the taking away from them their head."[15]

The great value Wesley placed upon the full involvement of women in the life of the early Methodist revival may also be seen in certain developments in London. Some of Wesley's followers there attempted to exclude women from a number of the society's activities. Their actions infuriated the founder. The injustice struck at the very root of the faith. "I do very exceedingly disapprove," Wesley informed the men, "of the excluding of women when we meet to pray, sing, and read the Scriptures."[16] These central acts of the Christian community were means of grace for all of God's children. It would ever remain so in Wesley's societies.

Many factors contributed to Wesley's early appreciation for women's gifts and the utilization of these gifts in the life of the church. Primary among these were the influence of his mother, the legacy of the Puritan heritage, his rediscovery of the practices of the early church, and his friendship with the Moravians. All contributed to the wider space given to women in the Methodist societies that were formed under the Wesleys' direction. The spirit of the Wesleys was one of both spiritual and social liberation. The Wesleyan revival within the Church of England was a barrier-breaking movement.

In the pages that follow, we will trace the expansion of women's leadership in early Methodism to the eventual acceptance of women as preachers within the movement. It was a painful process. Acceptance was slow in coming, but inevitable. The saga of the women preachers is an exciting story, a rich legacy. And in the telling of the story, history, theology, and personality merge to form a colorful tapestry, a testament to the truth of Christ. It is primarily because the ending of the story is not a happy one that the story must be told again and again. The Spirit who leads us into all truth can teach us from our past.

# Chapter 2

## *On the Cutting Edge of Revival*

### An Exclusively Female Sect?

John Wesley never intended to found a new denomination. He, and other like-minded clergy, formed small groups within the Church of England in order to rediscover a living faith rooted in love. These "religious societies" functioned as catalysts for renewal, like leaven within the loaf. They provided a supportive environment within which new disciples could explore their calling as Christians. Within these groups the early Methodists shared a life of faith working by love. The goal of their pilgrimage together was the prize of their high calling—conformity to Christ.

The heartbeat of the whole movement was personal religious experience and its power to transform both the individual and society. Wesley was ready to adopt and adapt any idea that might further this cause. His chief purpose was to help the Church proclaim the gospel more effectively. The spirit of the movement and the vision of the founder contributed both to the acceptance and encouragement of female leadership. Women pioneered and sustained the revival. Women, as well as men, were allowed to express themselves freely. They exercised their gifts in leadership. The small groups of the Methodist Society, known as bands and classes, became the training ground for the first women preachers.

For all intents and purposes, the Methodist Societies were organizations of women. Some critics even claimed that they were exclusively female sects. The same criticism had been leveled against the Quakers several generations before. And the opposition was equally harsh. A fellow clergyman indicted Wesley for keeping the women of Bristol so busy with religious work that they neglected their families. William Fleetwood dismissed the Methodists, or "Perfectionists" as he called them, as a group of "silly Women." James Lackington was more specific in describing them as "sour, disappointed old maids, with some others of a less prudish disposition."[1] Such attacks were unfounded, but the response of women to Wesley's liberating message was overwhelming indeed.

The preponderance of women in Methodism may be illustrated from Wesley's journal. At the outset of the revival, just two days after Wesley's first experience of preaching in the fields, he described the formation of a society in Bristol: "In the evening three women agreed to meet together weekly, with the same intentions as those at London—viz. 'to confess their faults one to another, and pray one for another, that they may be healed.' "[2] Several days later a second group was formed. A lot determined that Esther Deschamps would lead this exclusively female band of new disciples.

On Sunday, November 11, 1739, Wesley preached his first sermon in the ruins of an old foundry in London. Used originally for the production of canon, this building would later serve as headquarters for Wesley's spiritual crusade. When quarrels divided the religious society in Fetter Lane, Wesley reported the important consequences:

> Our little company met at *The Foundery*, instead of Fetter Lane. About twenty-five of our brethren God hath given us already, all of whom think and speak the same thing;

seven- or eight-and-forty likewise of the fifty women that
were in band desired to cast in their lot with us.[3]

A little more than two years later, in April 1742, Wesley
drew up the first list of the Foundery Society's sixty-six
leaders. In this significant group, women outnumbered the
men forty-seven to nineteen. A list of Select Society members in February 1744 reflects a similar proportion of fifty-
two women to twenty-five men. The example of the
Foundery Society with its 2:1 ratio of women to men is typical of early Methodism as a whole. While exclusively
female societies were rare, there can be no doubt that
women wielded tremendous influence during these formative years. Wherever Methodism was planted and flourished, women sowed the seed and gathered the harvest.

## We Trace Our Roots to Her

Of even greater significance than the preponderance of
women in the membership of the societies, however, is the
fact that women were conspicuous as pioneers in the establishment and expansion of Methodism. It was in large
measure due to the activities of women that the network of
societies under Wesley's direction quickly spread across
the land. Women invited and hosted the widening circle of
itinerant preachers. They founded prayer groups and societies on their own initiative. And their persistent labors
profoundly affected the general attitudes of Wesley and his
followers concerning their place within the movement.

When Wesley visited the neighborhood of Halifax in the
summer of 1742, Mrs. Holmes of Smith House, Lightcliffe,
invited him to preach at her home. Subsequently, Smith
House became a vibrant center of spiritual renewal. About
the same time, Wesley honored the request of a poor widow
in Chinley and made her home a resting place for his itinerants who began regular preaching there. Mary Allinson was
the first to open her house to Methodist preachers in Tees-

dale. The aunt of Mary Denny introduced Methodism to Maldon. Mrs. Hosmer procured a room for preaching in Darlington. Preaching was reinstated at Normanton only by means of an unnamed woman's persistence.

The famous stonemason preacher of the north, John Nelson, described typical events leading to the birth of Methodism in Leeds: "Now the people from every quarter have flocked to Birstal on the Sabbath, but as yet there came only three from Leeds,—Mary Shent and two other women."[4] Converted under the first sermon they heard, these "three Marys," including Mary Weddale and Mary Maude, formed the nucleus of the first band established in that strategic industrial center. And so it was in Ireland and Wales and throughout the counties of England.

Some women took the initiative in forming societies in their own communities. Several years before Wesley's first visit to Macclesfield, Mary Aldersley opened her home for religious services and was accustomed to meeting with her friends for prayer, reading of Scripture, and religious conversation. In 1746 Elizabeth Blow crossed the Humber River from Grimsby where she had been one of the earliest members and pioneered the founding of Methodism in Hull. Mrs. Martha Thompson, a wealthy widow from Rufforth, not only opened her own home for preachers, but used her influence to obtain their admission into the cathedral city of York.

Another Martha Thompson, of strikingly different background and circumstances from her namesake, is credited with the foundation of Methodism in Preston. With the assistance of Sarah Crosby, soon to be the first woman preacher of Methodism, Mrs. Dobinson of Derby became the principal organizer of a society there. In spite of tremendous opposition and frequent discouragement, these women pressed on toward their goals. In this pioneering work, a servant girl, a textile worker, or a housewife was no less acceptable than a woman of social position and influence.

One important contribution of wealthy women, however, was the construction of Methodist chapels. In Macclesfield, Elizabeth Clulow secured a small preaching house for the infant society. And when this chapel was soon outgrown, she oversaw the construction of a larger facility. Henrietta Gayer, wife of the clerk to the House of Lords for the Irish Parliament, was converted in 1772. The Methodist following in Lisburn quickly outgrew the "Prophet's Chamber," a room in her home set aside for preaching. She built the first chapel in that city, therefore, in 1774 and planned the construction of another in Donaghadee. In her widowhood she devoted the totality of her husband's estate to Christian work.

The first Methodist in Sevenoaks was Amy George. She had walked to Shoreham in order to invite Wesley to preach at her home. Wesley dedicated the chapel she built at the back of her business in 1774. He was impressed with the great hall which a Miss Harvey had built in her hometown of Hinxworth in Hertfordshire. In addition to this prominent center, she constructed several other chapels at her own expense in Baldock, Stevenage, and Biggleswade. She left a legacy of three thousand pounds to support their ministry at her death. Wesley held these pioneers and patrons in high esteem and valued their trust.

The pioneering work of Dorothy Fisher illustrates the way in which women stood on the cutting edge of the revival. Her influence was felt at every level of the society she founded. Converted under Wesley's preaching in London, she joined the society there in 1779. About the year 1784 she moved to Great Gonerby in Lincolnshire, opened her house to preaching, and in 1786 purchased a small stone building to serve as a chapel. A small group of Methodists at Sturton heard of Dorothy's piety and observed her work with tremendous excitement. They founded their hopes for a religious awakening at Lincoln in her.

The prime mover for this missionary venture, Sarah Parrot of Bracebridge, walked twenty-seven miles to Mrs.

Fisher's home. She boldly proclaimed that Dorothy had been brought to their area by God in order to bring Methodism to Lincoln. Concluding that it must be a call from God, Dorothy consented, settled her affairs, moved to Lincoln, purchased a large home to accommodate preaching, and invited the traveling preachers to make it their base of operations. Wesley, learning of the developments, expressed his hopeful expectations in a letter to his preacher, Lancelot Harrison:

> I am glad sister Fisher is settled in Lincoln, and that you have begun preaching there again. Hitherto it has been
> A soil ungrateful to the tiller's toil; But possibly it may now bear fruit.[5]

Dorothy formed a small society in an old lumber room near Gowt's Bridge. Not unexpectedly, it consisted of four women. And this newly planted society did begin to bear fruit. Dorothy built a chapel with an adjoining residence, all of which was deeded to the Methodist Conference. Thus Methodism was established in that cathedral city as it had been planted in many other places throughout the British Isles.

The faithful service of women such as Dorothy Fisher often gave them working equality with their male counterparts. But other actions also bonded the women to the hearts of their co-workers. Not only did the women serve, they also bore witness to their faith. Particularly in the early years of the revival, they had to learn, with Wesley, how to stare an angry mob in the face. That took courage. And perhaps nothing else had a way of gaining the respect of men more rapidly.

Following the Wednesbury riots of 1743, Wesley asked Joan Parks if she was frightened when the mob took hold of her:

> She said, "No; no more than I am now. I could trust God for you, as well as for myself." . . . I asked if the report was

true that she had fought for me. She said, "No; I knew God would fight for His children."[6]

When the mob attacked John Healy as he began to preach in the Irish village of Athlone, an unnamed Methodist woman swore that no one would harm this man of God. In spite of continued whippings that afterwards led to her death, she stood guard over the evangelist until help finally came. Hannah Davenport was more aggressive in the face of violence. When a mob attempted to force its way into her home where she was protecting Thomas Hanby, she seized an axe, stood in the doorway, and declared she would cut down the first person who dared to approach. Her method may have been crude and dangerous. Some might condemn her actions as less than Christian. There is no question, however, that she endeared herself to the Reverend Hanby that day.

## Caution Among the Ministers

In spite of the pervasive influence of women in this early period of the revival, both in witness and service, women were not allowed to preach in the Methodist societies. Wesley's primary concern was for evangelicalism to thrive as a reforming movement within the life of the Church. His allegiance to Anglicanism was an essential aspect of his character and self-understanding. In spite of his pressing concern for renewal, it was very difficult for Wesley to deviate from the practices and prohibitions of the Church he loved. His method was always to work from within as long as that was possible. While many of his discoveries were renewing the life of the Church, he moved with caution into areas that others might consider to be too innovative.

Wesley's early conservatism aside, one of the charges leveled against the Methodists during the first decade of their existence was the acceptance of women preachers. The Reverend William Bowman, one of Wesley's more vocal opponents, castigated the "enthusiasts" for this innovation in a pamphlet entitled *The Imposture of Methodism Display'd:*

> A Third Mark of Imposture propagated by these mad Devotionalists is their teaching, that it is lawful and expedient for mere laymen, for women, and the meanest and most ignorant mechanics, to minister in the Church of Christ, to preach and expound the Word of God, and to offer up the prayers of the congregation in the public assemblies.[7]

Other antagonists criticized Wesley for allowing some of his followers in London to associate with the radical French Prophetesses. Ironically, the fanaticism of these women frightened the Wesleys as much as their critics. Charles was repulsed by an encounter with one of these visionaries who "lifted up her voice like a lady on the tripod, and cried out vehemently, 'Look for perfection; I say absolute perfection!' and then concluded with an horrible hellish laugh."[8]

John simply cautioned the women and admonished them to "try the spirits to see whether they were of God." Both John and Charles, however, feared the destructive power of guilt by association. In 1743 Charles put his foot down and forbade the "speaking" of a woman in the Methodist gatherings at Evesham: "The Society walk as becometh the Gospel. One only person I reproved; not suffering her any longer, notwithstanding her great gifts, to speak in the church, or usurp authority over the men."[9]

John reflects the same conservative attitude in some of his writing from this period. He frequently discusses some of the controversial issues surrounding the revival. He corrects the mistaken impressions of his critics. He dissociates himself in principle and practice from "sects" that he felt were destructive to the life of the Church. His intention was to build and not to tear down. He wanted to adhere to the laws and regulations of his Church, and these included the restriction of women.

In two specific documents, Wesley disproves allegations

concerning women preachers within his movement. He demonstrates his opposition to women taking such a monumental step. The first of these pamphlets addresses his relationship to the Society of Friends. It was natural for the people of Wesley's day to associate the Methodists with the Quakers. Similarities between these two important movements were striking. In 1748, however, Wesley published an open letter to explain their differences. And one practice in particular, maintained Wesley, clearly distinguishes the Methodists from this "sect," namely, the preaching of women.

He rejects the Quaker notion that women have the right to preach in the assemblies of God's people. In defense of prohibition, he marshals the two classic Pauline texts, 1 Corinthians 14:34-35 and 1 Timothy 2:11-12, both of which appear to demand that women remain silent in church. He describes the "public teaching" of women as a usurpation of male authority. He uses standard arguments to counter Quaker defenses based on Scripture:

> "But a woman 'laboured with Paul in the work of the gospel.'" Yea, but not in the way he had himself expressly forbidden.
> "But Joel foretold, 'Your sons and your daughters shall prophesy.' And 'Philip had four daughters which prophesied.' And the Apostle himself directs women to prophesy; only with their heads covered."
> Very good. But how do you prove that prophesying in any of these places means preaching?[10]

Wesley may seem to be playing with words here, but his position is clear. He refused to allow the public preaching of women.

A second document relates to this issue as well. In the exchange of letters between Wesley and George Lavington, Bishop of Exeter, he responds to his superior's charge of enthusiasm. This was the constant outcry against his movement. The activities of women were used as evidence to support the charge. "Women and boys," charges Lavington, "are actually employed in this ministry of public preaching."[11] Wesley summarily dismisses the allegation, which was reminiscent of William Bowman's earlier charge. "Please tell me where?" he retorts. "I know them not, nor even heard of them before."[12]

Quibbling over the accuracy of the charge was hardly the point. There was more at risk. The cat-and-mouse game they played was only the tip of the iceberg. Lavington was simply functioning as a mouthpiece for those who feared the liberating and destabilizing influence of the Methodist Societies. The world of order and power, upon which leaders within the establishment based their own security, was showing signs of weakness. The evangelical revival, in conjunction with many other social forces, was beginning to change their world. In defense of the status quo, therefore, critics such as Lavington and Bowman used whatever means they had to stem the tide. They caricatured their "adversaries" and created stereotypes in which women often figured prominently. "'Tis observable in fact," claims the bishop, "that a multiplicity of wives, and promiscuous use of women has been the favorite tenet of most fanatical sects!"

Nothing, however, could have been further from Wesley's vision of the Christian life. His mission was to reform the Church. One unexpected consequence of his rediscovery of the gospel was the liberation it brought to all people, not just to women. While the women, at this point, were not allowed to preach, they were permitted to assume important positions of leadership within the Methodist Societies. They functioned as pioneers and often assumed working equality with men. And this is what the guardians of both church and society so greatly feared. The extraordinary nature of the revival, the general environment of the societies, and Wesley's evolving theology of the church and ministry, all led to even wider acceptance of women and the expansion of their roles.

# Chapter 3

## She Led the Way to Zion

### Influencing the Institution from Inside

The lay pioneers who founded many of the original Methodist Societies naturally assumed positions of leadership within the movement. Those who stood on the fringe of English society often found their way to the center of the Wesleyan revival. Methodism created its own leadership from within. It empowered the masses of working class and common people, and women, and trained them to be effective servants of the Word.

Wesley exhorted his followers to put apathy aside and to accept the responsibilities of their unique callings in Christ. He encouraged them to express their faith in works and to develop their talents as a sacred trust from God. He placed them in small groups in order to discover and nurture these gifts. This rediscovery of lay ministry contributed greatly to the inclusiveness and vitality of the movement. By allowing women to assume important positions of leadership within the Society structure, Wesley gave concrete expression to his proclamation of freedom in Christ. Women who were otherwise disenfranchised in a world dominated by men, began to develop a new sense of self-esteem and purpose.

By the close of the 1740s, leaders of the revival had

weathered the initial blasts from angry mobs and antagonistic clergy. In the process, they had also become more sensitive to the tension between their zeal for renewal and their loyalty to the Church. Methodism began to take shape as an institution. Specific levels of leadership began to emerge within the structure of the Societies. And Wesley, in his own unique and methodical way, brought clear definition to each of the roles as they evolved.

In addition to the "Ministers" (a rather small group of Anglican clergy at the top) and the "Assistants" or "Helpers" (a large group of itinerant lay preachers who devoted full time to the revival) were the lay leaders within the local Societies. Wesley placed his highest priority upon the cultivation of leadership within this vast army of disciples. Without the commitment and support of these grass-roots leaders, the revival could have dissolved quickly into a rope of sand. This third and largest group of leaders included the local, or non-itinerating preachers, conveners of the small groups, visitors of the sick, stewards, and housekeepers. It was within this crucial circle of leadership that the women found their widest range of opportunities. The offices of band and class leader and sick visitor proved to be most significant as training grounds for the later women preachers.

Wesley subdivided his Societies into small, homogeneous groups of four or five persons of the same sex and marital status. These "bands," as they were called, were intimate circles of fellowship for those "pressing on to perfection." Their central purpose was intense personal introspection and rigorous mutual confession. The "classes," generally composed of twelve persons of both sexes, had a practical origin. They developed in Bristol as logical divisions within the Society for the collection of money. Wesley seized upon this financial necessity as an opportunity to improve the pastoral care and oversight of his followers. The classes usually met weekly for fellowship of a somewhat less intensive nature than that of the bands.

Wesley appointed those persons under him who were responsible for the spiritual direction of these small groups. The band and class leaders stood nearest to the rank and file of the movement. They occupied strategic positions of leadership within the Societies. They exerted a powerful influence upon the development of the Methodist institution. The fact that these leaders were drawn from every conceivable sector of English society brought breadth and strength to the movement as to no other institution. Methodism not only survived but flourished because of this vast network of trained, functioning laypersons. These were not passive Christians for whom ministry was performed; rather, they were active, ministering servants who cared for one another. And most of them were women.

The band leaders, in particular, had to be persons of spiritual depth and maturity. Special gifts and qualities of character were necessary for the pastoral oversight of souls. Wesley required that his band leaders have a clear understanding of God's saving grace and the way of salvation. They had to be able to communicate their own experience and knowledge to others. Trustworthiness and personal integrity were indispensable qualities. The primary function of these leaders was to assist their Methodist brothers and sisters in a common quest for holiness. Many of the women were well suited by nature for this kind of spiritual nurturing. Indeed, some of them exercised their office with such sensitivity and discernment that the preachers refused to allow them to resign.

The class meeting was normally a kind of "family" gathering, where old and young, women and men, enjoyed fellowship together. It provided an opportunity for committed Christians to share their experiences, hopes, and dreams. Mutual accountability was the key to its success. It enhanced the life of the members and brought maturity to their faith. The class meeting was a safe place where caring members affirmed their triumphs, accepted their doubts, and assisted one another through the struggles of their journey. Everyone, women as well as men, was encouraged to "speak freely" within this circle of friendship concerning their Christian pilgrimage.

Those who were called upon to lead classes often found their lives changed dramatically by the experience. The responsibilities of directing others in matters of spiritual formation had a way of drawing out their own best qualities. According to Wesley, Jane Muncy, a class leader in London, was a "pattern to the flock." In "self denial of every kind, in openness of behavior, in simplicity and godly sincerity, in steadfast faith, and in constant attendance on all the public and private means of grace," she was a model to all. It is not surprising that many of the women were recognized widely for the breadth of their knowledge and the depth of their wisdom.

In those Societies that were large enough to have some degree of segregation, rarely was a man, apart from the preacher, allowed to lead an exclusively female class. On occasion, however, women found themselves as the leaders of men. When Dorothy Downes was drafted into such an arrangement in 1776, she turned to Wesley for his advice. Since her calling was of God, he charged her to lose no opportunity for doing good and to care for her brothers:

> As to the question you propose, if the leader himself desires it and the class be not unwilling, in that case there can be no objection to your meeting a class even of men. This is not properly assuming or exercising any authority over them. You do not act as a superior, but an equal; and it is an act of friendship and brotherly love.[1]

Sarah Crosby changed many people's lives by means of her leadership within these small groups. Honored as Methodism's first woman preacher, she built the foundation of her subsequent ministry upon these early experiences. From Frances Pawson's account of her leadership, it is easy to see how the small groups helped pave the way for the enlarged activity of women: "I cannot repeat all the good things I heard from Mrs. Crosby, Mrs. Downes, and others. I can only add, that those little parties, and classes, and bands, are the beginning of the heavenly society in this lower world."[2]

Another office in which the early Methodist women excelled was that of sick visitor. In a letter to his brother, dated April 24, 1741, Wesley describes the institution of this office in London: "I am settling a regular method of visiting the sick. . . . Eight or ten have offered themselves for the work, who are like to have full employment." In his lengthy letter of 1748 to the Reverend Vincent Perronet, later published as *A Plain Account of the People Called Methodists,* he describes the office in greater detail:

> It is the business of a Visitor of the sick, to see every sick person within his district thrice a week. To inquire into the state of their souls, and to advise them as occasion may require. To inquire into their disorders, and procure advice for them. To relieve them, if they are in want. . . . Upon reflection, I saw how exactly, in this also, we had copied after the primitive Church. What were the ancient Deacons? What was Phebe the Deaconess, but such a Visitor of the sick?[3]

While it was not their privilege to teach in public, these persons were called to be in ministry. Wesley's justification of their office elicited one of his most radical statements concerning women and the church. Not only were women to assume a working equality with men in matters of pastoral care, but their ministry was also a bold affirmation of the legitimate and noble place of women in the order of creation as well:

> "But may not *women,* as well as men, bear a part in this honourable service?" Undoubtedly they may; nay, they ought; it is meet, right, and their bounden duty. Herein there is no difference; "there is neither male nor female in Christ Jesus." Indeed it has long passed for a maxim with

many, that "women are only to be seen, not heard." And accordingly many of them are brought up in such a manner as if they were only designed for agreeable playthings! But is this doing honour to the sex? or is it a real kindness to them? No; it is the deepest unkindness; it is horrid cruelty; it is mere Turkish barbarity. And I know not how any woman of sense and spirit can submit to it. Let all you that have it in your power assert the right which the God of nature has given you. Yield not to that vile bondage any longer! You, as well as men, are rational creatures. You, like them, were made in the image of God; you are equally candidates for immortality; you too are called of God, as you have time, to "do good unto all men." Be "not disobedient to the heavenly calling." Whenever you have opportunity, do all the good you can, particularly to your poor, sick neighbour. And every one of *you* likewise "shall receive *your* own reward, according to *your* own labor."[4]

Leadership in these areas provided countless opportunity for women to discuss matters of faith, to counsel fellow travelers, to explain biblical insights, and to offer Christ to others by means of casual conversation and exhortation. When the visitation of the sick gradually and naturally expanded to include work in the prisons, women pioneered the way. When they offered their personal testimonies, read Scripture, and exhorted the inmates to receive God's love in Christ, how could Wesley disapprove? On the contrary, he encouraged them to do more.

## Grace Murray: The Model Leader

In this early period, Grace Murray stands out as a model of the Methodist woman. Her stature as one of the celebrities of early Methodism demonstrates the heights to which a woman could rise within the movement. She first appears in connection with the Foundery Society in London, where she is listed as one of the band leaders in 1742. Her *Memoirs* illustrate the typical experience of an early

Methodist woman: "Mr. Wesley made me a Leader of a Band; I was afraid of undertaking it, yet durst not refuse, lest I should offend God. I was also appointed to be one of the Visitors of the Sick which was my pleasant work."[5]

Returning to the north of England after her husband's death, she was appointed one of the first class leaders of the newly established Society at Newcastle. She entered into the pioneering work with unbridled zeal:

> Mr. Wesley fixed me in that part of the work which he thought proper; and when the House was finished, I was appointed to be the Housekeeper. Soon also, the people were again divided into Bands, or small select Societies; women by themselves, and the men in like manner. I had full a hundred in Classes, whom I met in two separate meetings; and a Band for each day of the week. I likewise visited the Sick and Backsliders. . . . We had also several Societies in the country, which I regularly visited; meeting the women in the day time, and in the evening the whole society. And oh, what pourings out of the Spirit have I seen at those times! It warms my heart now while I relate it.[6]

Her role quickly expanded to include even greater responsibilities. "She travelled," according to her son, "by Mr. Wesley's direction, through several of the northern counties, to meet and regulate the female societies; afterwards she went over into Ireland for the same purpose."[7] Vigilant in these itinerant labors, frequently traveling great distances without any companion, she quickly gained a reputation, not only for her pastoral skills, but for her courage as well. While an early historian of Methodism in the north asserts that "she never indeed attempted to preach," he affirms that Wesley was accustomed to speak of her as his "right hand."[8]

In the important document concerning his relationship with Grace, Wesley highly commends her work: "I saw the work of God prosper in her hands. . . . She was to me both a servant and friend, as well as a fellow-labourer in the Gospel."[9] Her various responsibilities as band and class leader, visitor of the sick, housekeeper, traveling companion, and itinerant "regulator" of the women's groups, all of which entailed no small amount of care and sensitivity, she discharged with zeal and fidelity. Women, such as Grace Murray, functioned, in effect, as sub-pastors, leading the Methodist family in their simple acts of worship and service.

## Wesley Makes Concessions

Wesley's theology of the church and his understanding of lay ministry provided the necessary foundation for his subsequent authorization of women preachers. That acceptance came, however, through a process of measured steps. It was a slow, but natural progression. Methodist practices modified Wesley's theology, and new theological insights led to innovative practices. Wesley's own self-understanding—his evolving view of his own role in the revival—played its part in the developments, too. The Wesleyan revival was extraordinary; and Wesley clearly recognized the exceptional nature of his own position.

Just three months after John began the practice of field preaching, he sought to justify his actions to his anxious brother: "And to do this I have both an ordinary call and an extraordinary. . . . Perhaps this might be better expressed in another way. God bears witness in an extraordinary manner that my thus exercising my ordinary call is well-pleasing in his sight."[10] The bishop confirmed his ordinary call on behalf of the Church; the Holy Spirit validated his extraordinary ministry on behalf of God's people.

The fact that spiritual fruits accompanied Wesley's novel activities in an extraordinary situation was proof enough for him of divine blessing. Wesley, the Anglican priest in earnest, was not stretching his credibility at this point. The most influential of Anglican theologians, Richard Hooker, had expressed this same view in his *Laws of Ecclesiastical*

*Polity.* But this basic conception, suppressed to a large extent by Wesley's day, was to have far-ranging implications. It could be applied directly to the practice of lay preaching, which developed during the first two decades of the revival. More importantly, it would supply the basic rationale for the inclusion of women in these fruitful activities in later years.

In these early decades, however, a tension existed in Wesley's mind concerning the nature of the church. His lifelong endeavor was to balance two fundamentally different views. The balancing act was a difficult one to master. On the one hand, the Church of England represented the apostolic or institutional church. Tradition linked it to its origins in Christ. The Wesleyan Societies, on the other hand, embodied a charismatic view of the church, using that term in its broadest sense. This view emphasized the faithful remnant, a fellowship of believers, a living faith held in the common experience of the few. So long as the Methodist Societies remained within the Church of England, Wesley could enjoy the best of both worlds. He enthusiastically embraced the truth in both views.

As early as 1746, however, Wesley tended to view the church more and more in essentially functional rather than institutional terms. Both structure and spirit, he believed, were necessary; but it is the Spirit that the structure embodies that is essential. Nowhere is this conviction more clearly expressed than in his important correspondence with the pseudonymous John Smith:

> I would inquire, What is the end of all ecclesiastical order? Is it not to bring souls from the power of Satan to God? And to build them up in His fear and love? Order, then, is so far valuable as it answers these ends; and if it answers them not it is worth nothing. . . . Wherever the knowledge and love of God are, true order will not be wanting. But the most apostolical order where these are not is less than nothing and vanity.[11]

The free and independent spirit of Susanna Wesley lived on in her son in such views. Many of Wesley's contemporaries perceived the seeds of nonconformity at their foundation.

Critics of the Wesleyan revival pointed to the early appearance of lay preachers within the Methodist Societies as the first indication that the seeds of dissidence had taken root. Lay preaching was a logical and natural extension of the egalitarian spirit of the Societies and the implicit theology of the movement. Wesley's field preaching was probably more "irregular" in a technical sense, but the invasion of parishes by unordained preachers was a perennial thorn in the flesh of Anglican clergy.

The origin of the lay preachers demonstrates Wesley's pragmatic churchmanship. He accepted the services of laypersons as leaders within the Societies without hesitation. Even in Georgia he had committed pastoral responsibility to gifted laypeople. But his assent to the activities of Methodist lay preachers depended upon the "extraordinary" nature of the revival. Wesley made this abundantly clear in his famous sermon "The Ministerial Office," in which he described the itinerant lay preachers of the 1740s as "extraordinary messengers, raised up to provoke the ordinary ones to jealousy." Extraordinary circumstances demanded unusual action and response.

Wesley justified his use of unordained preachers, not only in the divine mandate to proclaim salvation in Christ, but also as a pastoral necessity for his expanding movement. The "Ministers" simply could not keep pace with the explosive effects of the revival. While the early lay preachers drew their authority directly from Wesley, the response of the people and the fruit of their labor increasingly authenticated their ministry. This principle of self-authentication contributed greatly to the evolution of their ministerial self-consciousness.

The aspiring lay preachers, however, did have to meet Wesley's stringent requirements. The Conference of 1746 developed a three-fold test for those who felt that they were called to preach. Those who produced evidence of conversion or grace, gifts, and fruit were placed "on trial" for a period of one year. Following this time of "probation," if they succeeded in meeting the expectations of the Conference, they were admitted into "full connection." The essential qualification for these lay preachers, however, was a "call." And the authenticity of their call was tested by the fruit of their ministry.

While the call to preach ordinarily consisted of an inward call from God and an outward call of the church, the inner testimony of the Holy Spirit was always primary for Wesley. "I allow, that it is highly expedient, whoever preaches in His Name should have an outward as well as an inward call," he emphasized in his *A Caution against Bigotry,* "but that it is absolutely necessary, I deny." He took the argument one step further in response to the criticism of a fellow priest:

> It is true that in ordinary cases both an inward and an outward call are requisite. But we apprehend there is something far from "ordinary" in the present case. And upon the calmest view of things, we think they who are only called of God, and not of man, have more right to preach than they who are only called of man, and not of God.[12]

There was a certain sting in Wesley's words that could not be avoided.

God was not limited, you see, to the rules of the Church in Wesley's view. While God generally operates through the means—the ordinary channels ordained by Christ— God can never be bound to them alone. When the normal pastoral system fails to bear fruit, God raises up messengers to do what must be done. This, Wesley argued, was the extraordinary situation of his own day. And he used the soundest argument from Scripture, tradition, reason, and experience in order to build his case.

The profound influence that Susanna Wesley exerted

upon her son at this critical point must not be lost. Thomas Maxfield was the first Methodist lay preacher to be recognized and authorized by Wesley. John's initial revulsion at the thought of an unordained person expounding the Word was tempered and then transformed by Susanna's wise counsel:

> John, you know what my sentiments have been. You cannot suspect me of favouring readily anything of this kind. But take care what you do with respect to that young man, for he is as surely called of God to preach as you are. Examine what have been the fruits of his preaching: and hear him also yourself.[13]

As John listened, he could not help recalling a childhood memory of his own mother, surrounded by earnest seekers of God's grace, in the forekitchen of the Epworth rectory.

The fruit of which Susanna spoke was not dependent upon the Church's stamp of approval. Indeed, the fruit itself was equivalent to the sanction of the Church. While the "pastor" presided over the flock and administered the sacraments, it was the special province of the "evangelist" to assist him and preach the Word. Viewed as "prophets/evangelists," and not as "pastors/priests," the Methodist itinerant preachers were free to sow the seed of God's grace wherever the Spirit moved them to do so. Under Wesley they were to have a certain amount of freedom, but it was a liberty within the disciplined context of the Methodist Societies. Mutual accountability oftentimes held them on their course when the natural distractions of a "free lance" ministry would pull them afield.

Wesley's selection of these "sons in the gospel," as he called them, tended to evolve naturally. Candidates progressed by the logic of events from the lower levels of leadership in classes and bands, through a number of intermediate stages, to their eventual status as preachers. An anonymous critic illustrated this natural progression in his complaint: "No sooner does a person commence

Methodist; than he may hope to rise through all the different gradations of the Society, and may even aspire to become in time a travelling preacher."[14] Given the fact of female preponderance in the Societies, it is not surprising to find the same general pattern influencing the lives of women as well as men. The die was cast.

# Chapter 4

## *Did She Preach, or Not?*

The public speaking of women in Methodism took a number of forms preliminary to formal preaching. Three particular means of communicating their newly discovered faith took hold quite rapidly. While public prayer, testimony, and exhortation are distinct forms of public speaking, it was natural for them to overlap in the informal environment of the Methodist Society. Each of these forms of address was grounded in the desire to share the experience of faith and the urge to save souls. Not only could prayer easily become testimony, and testimony sound very much like exhortation, but any one of these means of communicating the gospel could transgress that fine line which separated them from preaching.

### She Began by Praying

For many of the early Methodist women public prayer was their first experience in public speaking. They were made to feel comfortable about praying in the small, family-oriented groups within the Societies. Quite often women founded prayer meetings to augment the classes and bands in which they participated. Their belief in the power of prayer is illustrated by the experience of Isabella

Wilson who became an important instrument of revival in the north of England:

> Hitherto, though urged to it, Miss Wilson had refrained from exercising herself publicly in the cause of religion, but hearing, from the late Mr. Percival, of the revival which had taken place in Yorkshire some years ago, in which it had pleased God particularly to own the prayer-meetings; and seeing her relations brought into Christian liberty, and the work prospering around her, from earnest supplications in private, she proceeded to pray more openly for such as were in distress of soul, and not in vain; the Lord often graciously answered for himself. Her mode of praying was not loud, yet fervent, and her faith remarkably strong in a present Saviour for a present salvation.[1]

The prayers of the women reflected a wide range of styles and forms. Wesley encountered an interesting specimen of prayer when his itinerary took him to Bath in 1764. In spite of its peculiarity, the prayer seems to have affected him greatly:

> The fire kindled more and more, till Mrs. — asked if I could give her leave to pray. Such a prayer I never heard before: it was perfectly an original; odd and unconnected, made up of disjointed fragments, and yet like a flame of fire. Every sentence went through my heart, and I believe the heart of every one present. For many months I have found nothing like it. It was good for me to be here.[2]

Many women were highly gifted in the art of prayer. It was said that Sarah Crosby could pray with the simplicity of a little child, and then rise to the language of a mother of Israel, proclaiming the deep things of God. Prayer was an art, mastered by women in the daily round of common events. Through prayer they were able to touch the lives of people in ways they could easily understand. Perhaps no woman of the eighteenth century was as skilled in this spiritual gift as Ann Cutler, affectionately known as "Praying Nanny."

Following her conversion Ann began to pray in public and through her experience became more and more convinced of her calling:

> She began to pray in meetings and several were awakened and brought to God. The effects of her labours were manifest. . . . Her manner and petitions were strange to numbers, as she prayed with great exertion of voice and for present blessings. She would frequently say, "I think I must pray. I cannot be happy unless I cry for sinners. I do not want any praise: I want nothing but souls to be brought to God. I am reproached by most. I cannot do it to be seen or heard of men. I see the world going to destruction, and I am burdened till I pour out my soul to God for them."[3]

Praying Nanny's public ministry was fruitful only because of the way in which she carefully balanced it with a personal devotional life of equal proportion. Time set aside for private meditation and contemplation provided the necessary foundation for an active mission in the world. Ann's concern for both contemplation and action, private and public discipline of the spirit, illustrates one of the dynamics that made the Wesleyan revival such a powerful force for God. She lived out Wesley's discovery that the Christian way is a life of prayer. Twelve to fourteen times each day, she stopped to give God thanks, to seek God's guidance, and to lift specific persons and situations into the healing presence of God's love. Her brothers and sisters knew what she was doing.

The work of Sarah Peters in the London prisons demonstrates how prayer often moved naturally into testimony and exhortation. Soon after John Wesley came to know Sarah, he noted how it was her "peculiar gift and her continual care, to seek and save that which was lost; to support the weak, to comfort the feeble-minded, to bring back what had been turned out of the way."[4] This band leader in the Foundery Society in London had a very clear sense of her special calling in life. "I think I am all spirit," she once said, "I must be always moving, I cannot rest, day or night, any longer than I am gathering in souls to God."

Sarah Peters and Silas Told were instrumental in the development of a ministry to the inmates of London's Newgate Prison. In October 1748 she assisted Silas in religious services for the condemned. The effects were dramatic:

> Six or seven of those who were under sentence of death came. They sung a hymn, read a portion of scripture, and prayed. Their little audience were all in tears. Most of them appeared deeply convinced of their lost estate. From this time her labours were unwearied among them, praying with them and for them, night and day.[5]

Sarah visited all of the prisoners in their cells. Going alone throughout the prison, she prayed with the inmates, offered them her personal testimony of God's love, and exhorted them to believe.

By means of her powerful ministry many were converted and bore witness to their newfound faith in the face of death. When John Lancaster, one of Sarah's first converts, entered the pressyard where his execution was to take place, she stood by his side to support him in his final hour. When the time came, he stepped to her, kissed her, and earnestly said, "I am going to paradise today. And you will follow me soon." His prophecy was fulfilled when, two weeks later, she died from "prison fever." A ministry cut short; an eternal legacy of love.

## Her Testimony Changed Lives

Personal testimony is rooted in the desire to share the liberating experience of new life in Christ with others. It is an unrestrained response to love one's brother or sister because God first loved us. Its ultimate purpose, therefore, is to change lives. True disciples of Christ simply cannot hide the joy they have experienced in him; they must pass on God's gracious gift to others. To hide Christ, as Wesley so frequently proclaimed, is to lose Christ in the end.

But testimony is also beneficial, if not essential, to personal spiritual formation. It can be used, not only to bring persons to Christ, but also to nurture them in the faith. Both aspects of the faith were ultimate concerns for Wesley. He recognized these dual dimensions of testimony and encouraged all of his followers to explore them fully. Far from introducing an innovation, Wesley simply rediscovered a neglected spiritual truth and promoted its use.

Testimony was, in fact, a significant religious tradition with deep roots in the Puritan notion of the "gathered church." It has always been central to those religious communities that value fellowship and mutual accountability, freedom of conscience and holiness as the goal of Christian life. Christians in pilgrimage together need to share their experiences along life's journey. And while Wesley never made the "testimonial of one's experience" a requirement for membership in the Methodist Societies (as was the case, for instance, in many of the churches with Puritan roots), the "giving of one's testimony" became a distinct feature of the Methodist gatherings.

It was natural, and therefore not uncommon, for the sharing of personal testimonies to immediately follow a regular service of preaching. During an extended tour of Wales, after preaching at Llansaintffraid, Wesley records that one of the women

> could not refrain from declaring before them all what God had done for her soul. And the words which came from the heart went to the heart. I scarce ever heard such a preacher before. All were in tears round about her, high and low; for there was no resisting the Spirit by which she spoke.[6]

Wesley's language is significant. The experience elicited his overwhelming approval because he saw God at work through this woman.

There were many occasions of public worship and Christian fellowship at which the testimony of women "pierced like lightning," as Wesley once said. The early morning preaching service, the love-feast, the watchnight service, and the covenant service provided the perfect context for such intimate sharing of one's struggles and triumphs in the faith. Of all these services, it was the love-feast that afforded women the greatest opportunity for self-expression.

The love-feast was really an extension of the class and band meeting. It was patterned after the *agape* meal of the early church and contemporary Moravian services. It was a very simple ceremony that could involve everyone in the symbolic act of eating and drinking together. The first Methodist love-feast was apparently held by a group of women, all members of the Society at Bristol, on April 15, 1739. As in all subsequent celebrations, the common meal was a powerful symbol of Christian family life. Prayer and singing were essential components of the experience. But the focal point was testimony, a spiritual sharing to which the meal was a symbolic prelude.

Usually held in the evening during Wesley's lifetime, the love-feasts sometimes lasted from 7:00 until 10:00 P.M. Bread or plain cake, and water in a loving cup, were passed around in a non-sacramental service that resembled Holy Communion in many ways. A whole body of hymnody developed around this special service. And the hymns emphasized the mutual ministry in which all were engaged:

> Let us join ('tis God commands),
> Let us join our hearts and hands;
> Help to gain our calling's hope,
> Build we each the other up.

There was no question about the ability of any person to speak in these gatherings as he or she felt led. The verse of a frequently sung hymn even enunciated the point:

Poor idiots He teaches to show forth His praise,
And tell of the riches of Jesus's grace.
No matter how dull the scholar whom He
Takes into His school, and gives him to see;
A wonderful fashion of teaching He hath,
And wise to salvation He makes us through faith.

The simplest of testimonies, filled with the Spirit of Christ, could be a powerful instrument of divine love. "I have seldom heard people speak with more honesty and simplicity," Wesley once wrote, "than many did at the love feast which followed. I have not seen a more unpolished people than these; but love supplied all defects."[7]

The supreme value of the love-feast for the women lay in its open fellowship and its Christian expression of freedom and equality. These were principles that Wesley was willing to fight for. At a love-feast in Birstal he reminded his followers of this very fact. "Many were surprised," he records with some concern, "when I told them, 'The very design of the lovefeast is free and familiar conversation, in which every man, yea, every woman, has liberty to speak.'"[8] In contrast to the intimate dialogue of the small fellowship groups, the love-feast provided a more public sphere for women to express their faith and develop their skills in speaking.

The joint meeting of the bands provided similar opportunities for women. One such meeting in Norwich proved to be quite a revival:

> While a poor woman was speaking a few artless words out of the fullness of her heart, a fire kindled and ran, as flame among the stubble, through the hearts of almost all that heard; so, when God is pleased to work, it matters not how weak or how mean the instrument.[9]

Likewise at Whitby, "one plain woman cried, and spoke, and cried again, so that they were in tears on every side."[10] Nothing, Wesley believed, could be of greater value for the nurturing of souls.

To share one's most intimate experiences in life takes great courage. While women in Wesley's day found it extremely difficult to break through the social barriers and offer Christ to others in this way, whenever they did, the sense of satisfaction it brought to their lives made it all worthwhile. The breakthrough of Jane Cooper, which came on January 15, 1762, reflects the experience of many other sisters in the faith:

> Went to Lon$^n$ on Friday to the Meeting. Mr. M$^d$ desired any to Speak who had not before declared the goodness of God. I was convinced I ought to Speak but fear'd I Sh$^d$ bring a reproach upon the Cause by my foolishness. Was tempted to think I sh$^d$ fall down in a fit if I began & that I knew not how to order my Speach aright. But the L$^d$ said "take no thou$^t$ how or what you shall Speak for in that hour it Shall be given you. . . .
> . . . I felt an awfull sense of God while Speaking & sat down with emotion that Spoak to my Heart, well don good & faithfull Servant. My Soul was so well Satisfied with the approbation of Xt. I neither wish'd nor fear'd what man thou$^t$ of me. I only pray'd they might receive the truth in the Love of it, lest their Souls Sh$^d$ suffer loss. I am content to be vile, let God be glorified & it sufficeth.[11]

Some of the men within the Society criticized Jane for the witness she bore. Such opposition was common in spite of Wesley's stand. For many, these activities transcended the limits of the sex. But Jane's mind was clear of offence. "Now I begin to be a deciple," she confessed, "if all men Speak evil of me for thy sake. Make me Steady to Stand reproach & give cause for it." The testimony of others, whose lives had been changed by her own life's story, was reward enough for Jane.

## Exhortation Bears Fruit

One of the intermediate stages between testimony and the public exposition of Scripture in preaching was exhortation. It consisted primarily of reproving sin, pleading for the sinner to repent and be saved, and testifying to one's own experience. Exhortation took a number of forms ranging from informal conversation in intimate circles to formal addresses in assembled groups. There was a natural progression in the sharing of one's "story" from testimony to urgent appeal. The small groups of early Methodism were specifically designed to encourage such activities. The most common form of exhortation, however, was that which followed the preaching of an itinerant in the informal services of the Methodist chapels.

Wesley emphasized the importance of direct, personal appeals in a letter to a young woman he felt was well-suited for the task:

> I believe you do not willingly lose any opportunity of speaking for a good Master. I apprehend you should particularly encourage the believers to give up all to God, and to expect the power whereby they will be enabled so to do every day and every moment. I hope none of your preachers speak against this, but rather press all the people forward.[12]

He advised another to "snatch all the opportunities you can of speaking a word to any of your neighbours." His constant plea was for all diligent Methodists, male or female, to "exhort the believers to go on to perfection."[13]

William Bramwell describes one of Ann Cutler's exhortations in some detail:

> In the evening we had a public prayer meeting in the chapel. She then stood upon one of the forms and gave us an exhortation, which was well approved. She was uncommonly earnest for precious souls. The zeal she had for them seemed to be unparalleled. There were many singularly blessed of God.[14]

Not only were hearers blessed in their hearing; exhorters received spiritual benefits as well. "One means of retaining the pure love of God," Wesley reminded Elizabeth Ritchie, "is the exhorting others to press earnestly after it. . . . I doubt not but this will be the chief matter both of your prayers and conversation. You may then expect to be more and more abundantly endued with power from on high."[15]

Words spoken at the close of life can powerfully impact the lives of the hearers. Wesley, therefore, encouraged "deathbed exhortations." These appeals were often recorded and, in time, developed into a distinctive genre of Methodist literature. "I should not wonder if a dying saint were to prophesy," exclaimed Wesley in a letter to his brother. "Listen to Sally Colston's last words!"[16] The record of Elizabeth Maxfield's final hour is exemplary:

> Some young people came to see her, and she exhorted them, very earnestly to turn to the Lord in the time of their youth. All were affected much, at what she said to them, as she let no one go out of her company without entreating them to trust in the Lord with all their hearts.[17]

While exhortations were common in the classes, bands, and prayer meetings, and occasionally served an evangelistic function outside the Societies, they most frequently followed the preaching of an itinerant. In this regard, Methodist "exhorting" was closely related to the Puritan "prophesying" of the previous century. The practice of Mary Holder, as recorded by Zechariah Taft, demonstrates their close relation:

> My method, as you know, was to give a word of exhortation after my dear husband had finished his sermon, or to pray, as I felt led by the spirit of God: and I must say, the Lord has owned and blessed my feeble efforts, to the spiritual profit of some precious souls.[18]

For most women, taking such a monumental step involved tremendous struggle. Many resisted the initial calling they felt into this ministry. Acceptance was the fruit of painful processes. Little wonder that many women desired to exhort in this manner only after some "friendly preacher" had ended his sermon. The experience of Sibyll Best illustrates the dilemma that many women faced:

> On her first obtaining the salvation of God, she felt much for sinners, and cried, and prayed for them before God in private. She saw it her duty now to pray for them and to exhort them in public; but the latter she felt, as if she durst not attempt; partly from natural timidity and bashfulness, and partly because she knew this would not be well received by some whom she thought she dared not to offend.[19]

Judith Land triumphed in her effort to reconcile an unequivocal sense of Christian responsibility with the social and religious norms of the day. But the struggle was painful:

> Feeling an increasing love for perishing sinners, and an earnest desire for their salvation, she ventured in public to give a word of exhortation, which the Lord owned with his blessing. She began to feel this more and more her duty: indeed the salvation of her own soul seemed closely connected with her striving to save the souls of others; she became alarmed at this. . . . She had no peace until she consented to exhort sinners to repent and turn to God: as soon as she obeyed God in this, her peace returned. She is never so happy as when exercising in these labours of love, knowing that this is the will of God concerning her.[20]

With the passage of time, exhortations (especially those following a sermon) assumed a somewhat rigid form. They were held together by the central thread of one's spiritual autobiography. In some isolated areas, for instance in Cornwall, local leaders established the office of "exhorter" in order to supply the lack of lay preachers or to augment their work. Some of these exhorters found themselves as permanent substitutes for seldom arriving traveling preachers. These leaders often made their evangelistic appeal by reading one of Wesley's sermons or some other selection of devotional material. Wesley had made the Christian classics available to them all very cheaply.

What distinguished the exhorter from the lay preacher was the "taking of a text." Preachers drew their message from a passage of Scripture. The practice, however, was not as clear cut as you might think, especially in an age when the language of the Bible filled the Christian's conversation. The distinction between preaching and exhorting was a fine one. And the fine line separating them could be crossed easily by an impassioned speaker, man or woman. At any rate, whether uttered as one's final appeal in the privacy of one's home, or shared as one's story of triumph in Christ within the context of a small group, or offered as words of wisdom by one matured in the faith for the benefit of her fellow pilgrims, each exhortation was one step closer to preaching. Women were speaking and being heard.

Alice Cross may have come close to transcending the fine line that separated exhortation from preaching. She introduced Methodism to Booth-Bank, Cheshire, in 1744. A pulpit was erected in the largest room of her house and a small Society formed. For many years she served as the leader of this small band of Methodists. She was well known for her philanthropic work and for the earnest way she appealed to her neighbors with regard to the faith. Because of her work, Booth-Bank became the center of Methodism in Lancashire and Cheshire. This "rude, uncultivated creature" with a "dash of the heroine in her," according to the description of Luke Tyerman, licensed her farmhouse for preaching even before a Methodist chapel was built in Manchester.

John Pawson left a remarkable manuscript account of her work. According to him, it was her practice to stand next to the pulpit to "declare the truth of Christ" whenever the itinerant preachers failed to make their appointed stop. This was a custom consistent with the practice of Quaker women preachers and other Dissenters of the previous century. Very seldom did women ever "enter the pulpit," especially when they were providing leadership in the absence of an expected preacher. Whether Alice technically preached is a question that can never be answered. At the very least, however, she functioned as an "exhorter" during a period of time in which male lay preachers within Methodism were an innovation.

In 1759, Wesley provided the following advice to a woman concerning the stewardship of her talents:

> In one word, be anything but a trifler, a trifler with God and your own soul. It was not for this that God gave you "a mind superior to the vulgar herd." No, Miss ———, no! but that you might employ all your talents to the glory of Him that gave them. O do not grieve the Holy Spirit of God! Is He not still stirring within you?[21]

If pushed to its logical end, the principle expressed in this statement could be used to sanction even the preaching of women. While the Wesleys could not yet accept such a step, the door was certainly ajar, and continuing to open.

Indeed, as early as 1755, and in spite of his general prohibitions, Wesley seems to allow for the possibility of women's preaching in exceptional cases. He finds his precedent in the practice of the early church: "Evangelists and deacons preached. Yea, and women when under extraordinary inspiration. Then both their sons and their daughters prophesied, although in ordinary cases it was not permitted to "a woman to speak in the church."[22] There was an increasing number of women who were ready to take the step. They were prepared to assume roles that had seemingly always been reserved for men. Even some of the men were willing to offer their pulpits to women preachers from outside their own tradition, such as Mary Peisley, a noted Quaker preacher from Ireland, who preached at the Norwich chapel in 1753.

The early Methodist women wanted to be faithful ambassadors for Christ. Their talents were being used in many ways within the life of the Methodist Societies. When pressed to defend their cause, they always had recourse to John Wesley's hymn:

> Shall I, for fear of feeble man,
> The Spirit's course in me restrain?
> Or, undismay'd in deed and word
> Be a true witness for my Lord?
>
> The love of Christ doth me constrain
> To seek the wandering souls of men;
> With cries, entreaties, tears, to save,
> To snatch them from the gaping grave.
>
> For this let men revile my name;
> No cross I shun, I fear no shame:
> All hail, reproach! and welcome pain!
> Only thy terrors, Lord, restrain.

# Chapter 5

 *Experimenting With or Without a Pulpit*

Samuel Johnson once remarked that "a woman's preaching is like a dog's walking on his hinder legs. It is not done well; but you are surprized to find it done at all." Unlike his noted contemporary, Wesley's initial prejudice against the preaching of women gradually melted away. Step by step, he followed the internal promptings of the Holy Spirit, always testing them with the authority of Scripture, reason, experience, and tradition. His attitude toward the whole question began to change over the course of the revival's third decade. From 1761 to 1770 the roles of women in the movement continued to expand in a logical and natural progression. While their numbers were never large, an influential group of women emerged as Methodism's first women preachers.

Had the question not arisen of its own accord, it is probable that Wesley would never have contemplated the use of women in preaching. Undoubtedly, the same could have been said with regard to the male lay preachers. As we shall see, Wesley's acceptance of the first women preachers followed the same pattern laid down a generation earlier in his response to the "extraordinary messengers" of the movement. Wesley never conceived of lay preaching, male or female, as a right to be seized. Rather, it was a gift of

God to an exceptional few to be exercised with a profound sense of responsibility.

## Sarah Crosby Receives Approval

While a number of early women came very close to preaching, the first woman to receive Wesley's authorization was Sarah Crosby. Unfortunately, very little is known about the early life of this significant figure. Born on November 7, 1729, apparently in the vicinity of Leeds, she was converted on October 29, 1749. One consequence of this transformation was a burning desire to proclaim her newfound faith to others. "I laboured to persuade all with whom I conversed," she says, "to come to Christ, telling them there was love, joy, peace, etc. for all that come to him."[1] She heard both Whitefield and Wesley preach in London during the winter of 1749, joined the Foundery Society in October of the following year, and was a well-established class leader by 1751.

Sarah's husband, the man who had introduced her to the writings of John Wesley, apparently deserted her after a marriage of about seven years, on February 2, 1757. A new chapter opened in Sarah's life the following May. She met Mary Bosanquet, with whom she formed one of the most significant alliances of early Methodism. Mary, a somewhat perplexed young lady at the time, sought the spiritual counsel of her Methodist friends. "I received a message from Miss Furley (now Mrs. Downs)," she later recalled, "that on such a day Mrs. Crosby would be at her house. I went to meet her in the spirit of prayer and expectation."[2] The simple way in which Sarah offered her testimony made them instant friends.

Later that summer Sarah settled in Christopher's Alley, in Moorfields, not far from the Foundery in London. There she lived with a circle of women that included Mrs. Sarah Ryan, Mary Clark, and occasionally her new friend, Mary Bosanquet. The work of these women among the poor and needy of London was soon to become famous. In later years, Mary often referred to this active community as her "little Bethel." Sarah found work among the poor to be exhilarating. Every person helped was a new friend in her eyes. She felt very much at home among those who made their faith the central occupation of their lives.

Activities in the London Society intensified her eagerness to exhort others to repentance and faith. Indeed, she seems to have been consumed by this sense of duty: "From the love I felt to those I knew to be equally fallen from original righteousness with myself, I often desired to be instrumental in turning them to God, and never had a moment's peace any longer than I endeavoured to aim at this wherever I came."[3] None of this is to say that religion came easy to Sarah. Her spiritual experience was characterized by perennial ups and downs. Her pilgrimage reflected the realities of life and the struggle to be faithful in her discipleship. But the more intimate her knowledge of salvation became, the stronger her desire to declare the work of God became.

After having assumed the responsibilities of a class leader she received a vision of Jesus while in prayer. The experience left a profound impression on her soul. Jesus spoke those words to her heart that he had spoken to Peter: "Feed my sheep." "Lord, I will do as thou hast done," she answered; "I will carry the lambs in my bosom, and gently lead those that are with young."[4] Other experiences soon confirmed her calling to become a shepherd of the sheep. Never satisfied with the hope of being "almost a Christian," as Wesley would say, she discovered the joy of being "altogether a Christian." "I am determined to be all the Lord's," she wrote in her letterbook during a period of profound religious awakening; "yea and My God hath taken me for His own forever."

She stood on the threshold of a new ministry. In 1761 a zealous new Methodist and her husband moved from London to Derby with the express intention of forming a

Methodist Society there. Sarah, excited by the prospect of such a thrilling adventure, offered her assistance. Twenty-seven people were present at the first class meeting on Sunday evening, February 1. Sarah was overwhelmed, and somewhat embarrassed by the events of the following week:

> Sun. 8. This day my mind has been calmly stayed on God. In the evening I expected to meet about thirty persons in class; but to my great surprise there came near two hundred. I found an aweful, loving sense of the Lord's presence, and much love to the people; but was much affected both in body and mind. I was not sure whether it was right for me to exhort in so public a manner, and yet I saw it impracticable to meet all these people by way of speaking particularly to each individual. I, therefore, gave out a hymn, and prayed, and told them part of what the Lord had done for myself, persuading them to flee from all sin.[5]

Sarah knew that she had come perilously close to preaching. She immediately wrote to her spiritual mentor seeking his advice. Wesley does not seem to have been unduly worried. He took his time in responding to her inquiries, although dispatched to him under a great sense of urgency. In the meantime, on Friday, February 13, Sarah addressed a large congregation once again. And the results further confirmed the resolve of her own mind:

> In the evening I exhorted near two hundred people to forsake their sins, and shewed them the willingness of Christ to save: They flock as doves to the windows, tho' as yet we have no preacher. Surely, Lord, thou hast much people in this place! My soul was much comforted in speaking to the people, as my Lord has removed all my scruples respecting the propriety of my acting thus publickly.[6]

The arrival of Wesley's letter brought further confirmation of her inner conviction:

London, February 14, 1761

My Dear Sister,

Miss Bosanquet gave me yours on Wednesday night. Hitherto, I think you have not gone too far. You could not well do less. I apprehend all you can do more is, when you meet again, to tell them simply, "You lay me under a great difficulty. The Methodists do not allow of women preachers; neither do I take upon me any such character. But I will just nakedly tell you what is in my heart." This will in a great measure obviate the grand objection and prepare for J. Hampson's coming. I do not see that you have broken any law. Go on calmly and steadily. If you have time, you may read to them the *Notes* on any chapter before you speak a few words, or one of the most awakening sermons, as other women have done long ago.[7]

This event, and Wesley's qualified approval of Sarah Crosby's actions, marks the beginning of his acceptance of women preachers. The more stringent aspect of Wesley's churchmanship made it impossible for him, at this point, to use the term "preacher" in such cases. His suggestion concerning the reading of Scripture or his notes on the New Testament, and then speaking to a large assembly, however, comes perilously close to preaching in a more technical sense. At any rate, Sarah took Wesley's advice concerning the practices of "other women long ago," an unmistakable reference to the activities of his own mother in the Epworth rectory, and on Good Friday, March 20, "read a sermon on the occasion to several persons, who were met together, and went to bed weary but happy in God."[8]

While Wesley seems to have told Sarah that it was all right to preach as long as she didn't call her activities preaching, it is clear that Wesley was still struggling to come to terms with specific biblical statements that were clearly prohibitive. As in all circumstances, his basic rule was to deal with each particular situation or person in the light of Scripture. He had a circumstance very similar to Sarah's to deal with in the experience of Grace Walton.

Although Wesley's letter to her has been damaged through the years, its message is pretty clear in this reconstructed form:

London, September 8, 1761

If a few more Persons come when you are meeting, you may either enlarge four or five Minutes on the Question you had or give a short Exhortation (perhaps for five or six minutes) and then sing & pray: This is going as far as I think any Woman should do. For the Words of the Apostle are clear. I think as always, that his meaning is this: "I suffer not a woman to teach in a public congregation, nor thereby to usurp Authority over the man."[9]

Wesley rigidly interprets Paul's directive to Timothy. Indeed, his note on 1 Timothy 2:13 goes so far as to say "that Woman was originally the Inferior." While Wesley's legalism with regard to 1 Corinthians 14:34 is clear and consistent, in his notation on this verse he admits the possibility of exceptions:

"Let your women be silent in the churches." Unless they are under an extraordinary impulse of the Spirit. "For," in other cases, "it is not permitted them to speak"—By way of teaching in Publick assemblies. "But to be in subjection"—To the man whose proper office it is to lead and to instruct the congregation.[10]

Would-be woman preachers would later point Wesley to his own words in defense of their labors.

## Mary Bosanquet and Her Little Family

The evangelical revival exploded in the early 1760s. In April 1761, Sarah Crosby returned from her pioneering work in Derby to contribute to the expansion of Methodism in London. A letter of January 28, 1763, reveals that she was fully employed throughout the latter half of the previous year:

I have been 5 months at Canterbury, wch has been much for my own good, & the good of many. there has been a great revival, & quickening among the peopel. when I have an Oppertunity, I will send you the Coppy of the account, Mr. W[esley] desired me write him.[11]

Her return enabled her to renew old friendships with Mary and her circle of female companions.

Mary was born into a wealthy family on September 1, 1739, at Leytonstone in Essex, outside of London. A servant girl in her household introduced her to Methodism at an early age. In spite of strong opposition from her family, she became involved in the Wesleyan Society. Shortly after her initial encounter with Mrs. Crosby, Mary met Mrs. Sarah Ryan. Sarah immediately took the young lady under her wing. "The more I conversed with Mrs. Ryan," Mary confided to her diary, "the more I discovered of the glory of God breaking forth from within, and felt a strong attraction to consider her as the friend of my soul."[12] While her parents spent their summer holiday in Scarborough in 1757, Mary immersed herself in the life of the Methodist Society.

Sarah Ryan, her newfound friend, was a leading spirit in the Foundery and one of Wesley's most intimate friends and faithful correspondents. Born of poor parents on October 24, 1724, she was stirred by the preaching of George Whitefield at seventeen years of age. After hearing Wesley in London she joined the Foundery Society and quickly progressed through the Methodist ranks. Experiences in her new spiritual home among the Methodists enabled her to triumph over her earlier years of deprivation. Wesley appointed her housekeeper in Bristol later in 1757, a position that demanded his full confidence and proved her exceptional maturity in the faith. Under her administration Kingswood School became "what I have so long wished it to be," said Wesley, "a blessing to all that are therein and an honour to the whole body of Methodists."[13]

Mary Bosanquet, however, was to become the guiding light in this close circle of friends and committed disciples of Christ. When her family hatred of Methodism became intolerable to her, Mary moved to Hoxton Square where she rented two unfurnished rooms. There she committed herself to a daring plan of ministry and service. She fixed her mind on the example of Christ and allowed nothing to distract her from a life of faith working by love. Mrs. Ryan returned from Bristol to offer her assistance and nurse her own declining health. In spite of her weakness, "Mary's twin soul," as Wesley called her, worked untiringly with her friend in this semi-monastic conclave.

In 1763 these two women expanded their ministry considerably. At this point they contemplated moving to "The Cedars," a large home in Leytonstone that had become vacant. Mary's father, who owned the property, made no objection. Only partially reconciled to Mary's new style of life, he brusquely concluded the transaction by saying: "If a mob should pull your house about your ears, I cannot hinder them." And so, on March 24, 1763, the wealthy and cultured Miss Bosanquet and Mrs. Ryan, former domestic servant, made the bold move to Leytonstone. Their dream was to establish an orphanage and school on the basis of Wesley's own prototype at Kingswood. It was a grand vision. No two people had better gifts for the work.

Wesley kept his eye on the model Christian community. It combined vibrant personal piety and active social service. Less than a year later Wesley expressed his high hopes and great expectations concerning its progress: "M[ary] B[osanquet] gave me further account of their affairs at Leytonstone. It is exactly *Pietas Hallensis* in miniature. What it will be does not yet appear."[14] It became a sanctuary for the most destitute and friendless of the London streets. In fact, Mary and Sarah decided to take in none but the least and last and lost in obedience to Christ's command.

The children who were chosen often came "naked, full

of vermin, and some afflicted with distemper." At first the family consisted of Mary, Sarah, a maid, and Sarah Lawrence, Mrs. Ryan's orphaned niece. With the addition of five more orphans and confronted with the problem of Mrs. Ryan's failing health, a pious young woman, Ann Tripp, was secured as a governess for the children. These women formed themselves into a tightly knit community. They adopted a uniform dress of dark purple cotton and all ate together at a table five yards long. Over the course of five years they sheltered and cared for thirty-five children and thirty-four adults. What in other hands might have become an elegant house became a school, an orphanage, a hospital, and a halfway house for some of London's most deprived people.

The foundation of this vibrant community of faith was disciplined prayer and study. Simple and informal acts of worship soon expanded beyond the expectations of the women involved in their leadership:

> In order to supply the want of public means, (which we could not have but when we went to London,) we agreed to spend an hour every night together in spiritual reading and prayer. A poor woman with whom I had formerly talked, came to ask if she might come in, when we made prayer. We told her at seven every Thursday night she should be welcome. She soon brought two or three more, and they others, till in a short time our little company increased to twenty-five. . . . Some few were offended, and came no more; but most appeared under conviction, and those we appointed to meet on Tuesday night, reserving the Thursday for the public meeting, which still kept increasing, and in which we read a chapter, and sometimes spoke from it.[15]

The women applied to Wesley for a preacher. Their plan was approved promptly. The following Sunday, Mr. Murlin preached, and within two weeks a new Society with twenty-five members was formed. The women, Mary and Sarah at first, continued their Thursday evening public services. These included the reading and exposition of Scripture. Opposition began to develop, but the women continued in this practice. Mary often addressed large assemblies which flocked to "The Cedars" in order to be fed with spiritual food. It may have been this growing tradition at Leytonstone, or the efforts of other women throughout Britain, that stirred the wrath of certain male colleagues at this point.

When the annual Conference of Wesley's itinerant preachers was convened in Manchester on August 20, 1765, one of the questions put before the leaders concerned the Pauline prohibitions related to the women. Wesley says no more than is absolutely necessary in his response to the question: "How can we encourage the women in the Bands to speak, since 'It is a shame for women to speak in the Church'?"

> I deny, 1 That speaking here means any other than speaking as a public teacher. This St. Paul suffered not, because it implied "usurping authority over the man." 1 Tim. ii. 12. Whereas no authority either over man or woman is usurped, by the speaking now in question. I deny, 2 That the Church in that text, means any other than the great congregation.[16]

In spite of the official position of the Conference, Sarah Crosby continued to expand her own itinerant ministries. Wesley apparently saw no need to restrict her activities. On the contrary, in his correspondence with her, his words are almost always words of encouragement. Prior to the Manchester Conference, Sarah set forth her own views on the subject of women's speaking in a letter to a friend, perhaps in anticipation of discussions there:

> I think I do use the little Strength I have in Instructing the Ignorant, reclaiming the wicked, relieving the Pain of those who suffer in body or mind. I am generely some way or other imployed in some of these works. I am not conscious of any willfull omissions. Lord correct me where I go

astray! Unless my not speaking amoung the [Brethren] may be stiled omissions However I broke through that Sometime agoe and been blesst in Speaking. I do not think it wrong for women to speak in public provided they speak by the Spirit of God.[17]

Sarah was so often on the go that it is difficult to determine exactly when she became connected with the Leytonstone orphanage and its work. As early as September 1766, however, Wesley was addressing letters to her at that address. From that point on, the lives of the three women, Mary and the two Sarahs, became inextricably intertwined. On February 12, 1767, Wesley was delighted with the effective ministry of the community. "Oh what a house of God is here!" he exclaimed. "Not only for decency and order, but for the life and power of religion!"[18]

In May of that year, somewhat displeased with Mrs. Crosby for not having heard from her in some time, Wesley wrote from Sligo, encouraging her to press on in her work: "I hope your little family remains in peace and love and that your own soul prospers. I doubt only whether you are so useful as you might be. But herein look to the anointing which you have of God, being willing to follow wherever He leads, and it shall teach you of all things."[19]

Shortly thereafter, Sarah and the entire Leytonstone family did, in fact, follow God's lead to an exciting new ministry. Mary had always dreamed of living on a farm and caring for her children in the quiet of the country. The burden of financial pressures, the deterioration of Sarah Ryan's health, and the appeal of a religious awakening in the north of England all pointed to the need for a change. A visit from Richard Taylor, and his offer to resettle the orphanage in Yorkshire, seemed to be a providential sign. On June 7, 1768, the "little family" set out for their new home, literally not knowing where they were going.

They made the arduous journey north to a strange land, wild and sparsely populated, with few roads and none of the comforts of civilization. Nevertheless, Yorkshire was one of the thriving centers of early Methodism. It boasted nearly one third of all the Methodist chapels by 1770. There were many kindred spirits to greet here. The small company stayed with Mrs. Taylor's parents until early August, at which time they found a suitable house at Gildersome in Yorkshire's West Riding. Mary's hopes that the change of air might benefit Sarah Ryan were dashed, however, on August 17, 1768, when her "twin soul" died at the age of forty-three. The original epitaph on her gravestone in Leeds Old Churchyard reflects the character and simplicity of one "Who lived and died a Christian."

The new home for the orphanage, a farmhouse appropriately named Cross Hall, soon became a vital center of Methodist worship and witness. Sarah Crosby had spent some time in Yorkshire previously, and several persons who had been affected by her words in the past now agreed to meet with them regularly at midweek for prayer. The ministry of the women, as usual, expanded beyond their wildest dreams:

> One and another begged to join in our Wednesday night meetings, and our number increased to about fifty, all of whom were ardently desiring, or sweetly brought into, that liberty. When we grew too numerous, (for they began to come from many miles round,) I advised those who were able, to gather a meeting of the same kind near their own homes. This was attended with many blessings. We sometimes visited those infant meetings, and they increased and spread as well as ours.[20]

Wesley, still very sensitive about the issue of women preachers, thought he had better provide the Cross Hall women with some clear-cut guidelines concerning their activities. He wrote to Sarah, therefore, from Chester on March 18, 1769:

> I advise you, as I did Grace Walton formerly, (1) Pray in private or public as much as you can. (2) Even in public

you may properly enough intermix *short exhortations* with prayer; but keep as far from what is called preaching as you can: therefore never take a text; never speak in a continued discourse without some break, about four or five minutes. Tell the people, "We shall have another *prayer-meeting* at such a time and place." If Hannah Harrison had followed these few directions, she might have been as useful now as ever.[21]

Wesley's position was clear. Just as he had advised the early lay preachers, now, some three decades later, he cautioned the women to avoid what appeared to be "preaching." The determining factors, as earlier, were "taking a text" and "speaking in a continued discourse." Wesley was clearly anxious about the activities of Sarah Crosby and Mary Bosanquet. Even though he was increasingly sympathetic toward their work, he was not yet prepared to radically modify his conservative views concerning their rights within the church. He still differentiated testimony and exhortation from formal preaching. He still believed that such a fine distinction would prevent the objection of the critics and safeguard the integrity of his movement. He should have known better, however, from his experience with the lay preachers. In the years that followed, Cross Hall, the headquarters for the pioneering work of women in the north, became the focal point for discussions related to this potentially volatile issue.

## Other "Blessed Women"

Other women sought to express their faith actively and openly. Hannah Harrison, the aspiring young preacher about whom Wesley voiced his disapproval, is a prime example. Described by Wesley at one point as a "blessed woman," Hannah developed a reputation as a gifted mediator with few peers. At her home in Beverley, she intervened on behalf of the itinerants, or Culamite preachers as they were called, who were so frequently besieged by furious mobs. "There seems to have been a particular providence in Hannah Harrison's coming to Beverley," Wesley observed, "especially at that very time when a peacemaker was so much wanting; and it was a pledge that God will withhold from you no manner of thing that is good."[22]

While many of the facts concerning her life will forever remain a mystery, Hannah was undoubtedly a native of York, having been born there in 1734.[23] She was converted under the preaching of Jonathan Maskew in November 1750 and shortly thereafter experienced a profound deepening of her faith at a celebration of the Lord's Supper. Next to nothing is known about her ministry. No reliable records of her activities have survived. But she was apparently instrumental in the establishment of Methodism in her native home, in York. There is some evidence of her having presided over numerous public meetings in nearby Malton. Perhaps it was here that her failure to comply with Wesley's "few directions" led to some punitive action on his part. We simply do not know.

Mrs. Eliza Bennis, who founded Methodism in Waterford, was the first of Wesley's followers in Limerick. She functioned for a number of years, in all but name, as Wesley's "Assistant" in Ireland. There can be no doubt that her responsibilities led her into countless situations that would have been conducive to preaching. Wesley encouraged her, for instance, to assume the office of a co-worker with Richard Bourke, one of his faithful Irish itinerants. To her he expressed his hope that they would "faithfully endeavour to help each other on." "Remember you have work to do in your Lord's vineyard," he reminded her, "and the more you help others the more your soul will prosper."[24]

Indeed, Mrs. Bennis actually supervised the activities of the circuit. In a letter of July 8, 1770, she advised Wesley:

> I hope you will not think me presumptuous in dictating, but I find my soul knit to these poor sheep. . . . Brother Bourke, at my request, has taken Clonmel into the circuit,

and doubt not but there will be good done there; but as this has caused an entire alteration in the circuit from the former plan, I have to request your forgiveness for my officiousness; if you disapprove, it can be re-altered.[25]

Far from castigating her for what some might have considered a flagrant usurpation of authority by a woman, Wesley fully approved her modification of the circuit plan and continued to seek her counsel on all such matters.

Later that same summer, Wesley was prohibited from preaching in a parish church because the congregation thought he had allowed a woman to preach at Huddersfield. The alleged preacher was none other than Sarah Crosby. While Sarah claimed only to have met a Class there and defended her actions to Wesley, the incident never even reached a level of concern in his own mind. He confided to Sarah that he had "places enough to preach in."

By the end of the summer of 1770, however, it was becoming increasingly clear that the question of women's preaching was an issue that required more immediate attention on the part of the Methodist leadership. Indeed, Sarah presupposed that "our Preachers will have it up at the Conference." She expressed her great interest to Mr. Mayer, as one might well expect, "Concerning what passes on that Head." Unfortunately, no record of the Conference's deliberations on this issue has been preserved. The role of women within the Wesleyan revival, and the particular status of aspiring women preachers, may have been clear in the minds of some Methodist leaders. No formal actions, however, were taken. Their future was still very much dependent upon the attitude of Mr. Wesley.

No matter how innocent, the radical implication of his advice to one young lady was blatantly obvious to the conscientious women who aspired to fulfill a strong sense of Christian vocation.

There is one rule which our Lord constantly observes,— "Unto him that hath shall be given." "Unto him that *uses* what he hath." Speak, therefore, as you can; and by-and-by you shall speak as you would. Speak, though, with fear; and in a little time you shall speak without fear. Fear shall be swallowed up in love![26]

Love is a powerful motivating force. For those who felt compelled to proclaim the reality of the love they had experienced in their lives, little was left to hold them back. If these women were, in fact, being called to preach, that call demanded clearer definition.

# Chapter 6

## Extraordinary Women for Extraordinary Tasks

As the evangelical revival wore on, Wesley found it increasingly difficult to reconcile the extraordinary dimensions of his Societies with the ordinary structures of the Church. Between 1771 and 1780 the advancing movement slid increasingly and inevitably toward independence. Wesley made every effort to march with the leaders of the religious establishment. He was an Anglican in earnest. He loved the Church with all his heart and remained faithful to it to the end of his life. But his eyes were so firmly fixed on his spiritual goal that he strayed far from the column.

Wesley's attitude toward the women preachers changed dramatically during this critical period. His experience with Sarah Crosby over the course of the prior decade paved the way for momentous decisions. He had moved cautiously, with measured steps, from discreet approval of her actions in Derby, to encouragement of exhortation, to qualified authorization of her fuller ministry. As he entered the 1770s, Wesley was prepared to take another full step—a step closer to the realization of his mission, a step further away from his beloved Church.

### Wesley Defines the Call

It became increasingly clear to Wesley that he must accept an occasional woman preacher by virtue of an "extraordinary call." The work of the Cross Hall women brought these developments to a head. During the summer of 1771, Mary Bosanquet wrote a lengthy letter to Wesley concerning their work in Yorkshire. It is the first serious defense of women's preaching in Methodism. Mary's letter is marked by sound and prudent judgment. She argues that, on the basis of her examination of Scripture, women were occasionally called of God to preach in extraordinary situations.

Cross Hall, near Leeds, 1771

Very dear and honoured Sir,

Various have been my hinderances in writing, but none sufficient to have kept me so long silent to you, had I not been at a loss on one particular subject. I want your advice and direction in an important point, and to know if you approve my light in it.

When we first settled at Laytonstone, sister Ryan and I began with little kind of prayer-meetings, etc., and they were productive of a blessing. Afterwards, on coming into Yorkshire, sister Crosby and I did the same—God was with us, and made it known by the effects in many places—but several object to them.

1st Objection. 2 Tim. ii. 12. "Let the women learn in silence," etc. I understand that text to mean no more than that a woman shall not take authority over her husband, but be in subjection, neither shall she teach at all by usurping authority, she shall not meddle with church discipline, neither order, nor regulate any thing in which men are concerned in the matters of the church; but I do not apprehend it means she shall not intreat sinners to come to Jesus, nor say, "Come, and I will tell you what God hath done for my soul."

2nd Objection. Nay, but the apostle says, 1 Cor. xiv. 34. "Let your women keep silence," etc. I answer, was not that spoke in reference to a time of dispute and contention? So that his saying, "they are not permitted to speak," here seems to me to imply no more than the other, she is not to meddle with church government?

3rd Objection. Nay, but it means literally not to speak by way of edification, while in the church, or company of promiscuous worshippers. Answer, Then why is it said, 1 Cor. xi. 5, "Every woman that prayeth or prophesieth with her head uncovered, dishonoureth her head." Can she prophesy without speaking? or ought she to speak, but not to edification?

4th Objection. She may now and then, if under a peculiar impulse, but never else. Answer, But how often is she to feel this impulse? Perhaps you will say, two or three times in her life. Perhaps God will say, two or three times in a week, or day; and where shall we find the rule for this?

5th Objection. But it is inconsistent with that *modesty* the Christian religion requires in *women* professing godliness. Answer, It may be, and is painful to it, but does not Christian *modesty* stand in these two particulars—*purity* and *humility*? 1st, I apprehend it consists in cutting off every act, word, and thought, which in the least infringes on the *purity* God delights in—2nd, In cutting off every act, word, and thought, which in the least infringes on *humility;* knowing thoroughly our own place, and tendering to every one their due; endeavouring to be little, and unknown, as far as the order of God will permit, and simply following that order, leaving the event to God. Now I do not apprehend *Mary* sinned against either of these heads, or could in the least be accused of *immodesty*, when she invited the whole city to come to CHRIST. Neither do I think the woman mentioned in 2 Sam xx, could be said to sin against *modesty*, though she called to the General of the opposite army to converse with her, and then went to all the people to give them her advice, and by it the city was saved. Neither do I suppose *Deborah* did wrong, in publicly declaring the message of the LORD and afterwards accompanying Barak to war, because his hands hung down at going without her.

6th Objection. But all these were extraordinary calls; sure you will not say, yours is an extraordinary call? Answer, If I did not believe so, I would not act in an extraordinary manner—I praise God, I feel him near, and I prove his faithfulness every day.

I am, etc.
M[ary] B[osanquet][1]

This letter impressed Wesley greatly. It elicited a definitive statement from Mary's spiritual guide. In his response,

Wesley defends the legitimate nature of her unique calling. He affirms an apostolic precedent both for her "innovative" activities and for Methodist irregularities in general:

Londonderry, June 13, 1771

My dear sister,

I think the strength of the cause rests there, on your having an *Extraordinary Call.* So, I am persuaded, has every one of our Lay Preachers: otherwise I could not countenance his preaching at all. It is plain to me that the whole Work of God termed Methodism is an extraordinary dispensation of His Providence. Therefore I do not wonder if several things occur therein which do not fall under ordinary rules of discipline. St. Paul's ordinary rule was, "I permit not a woman to speak in the congregation." Yet in extraordinary cases he made a few exceptions; at Corinth, in particular.[2]

In an accompanying letter to Sarah Crosby, Wesley suggests that she "take a text" whenever she is called upon to address a large gathering. The final obstacle to formal preaching was thereby removed. "Making short observations," Wesley continues, "may be as useful as any way of speaking."[3] In a subsequent letter he clearly addresses Sarah as a co-worker with Christ in their common ministry: "I hope you will always have your time much filled up. You will, unless you grow weary of well doing. For is not the harvest plenteous still? Had we ever a larger field of action? And shall we stand all or any part of the day idle? Then we should wrong both our neighbour and our own souls."[4] In this same piece of correspondence, Wesley reiterates the principle of an "extraordinary call." While the Quakers flatly deny the rule established by Paul, he maintains, "We allow the rule; only we believe it admits of some exceptions."

For this very reason, some women defected to the Society of Friends. The first woman preacher to take this course of action was Mary Stokes, a trusted Methodist leader at Bristol. The Quaker historian Rufus Jones has described her as "one of the greatest and most influential of the women preachers of the eighteenth century."[5] She possessed remarkable gifts for ministry. Her preaching was balanced and vibrant. In every sermon she attempted to communicate both what Christ has done for us and what the Spirit is doing within us. The dynamic quality of her preaching—a legacy she carried with her from her Methodist past—struck a new note in Quaker preaching. Methodism's loss was Quakerism's gain.

Wesley, in fact, never did take that final step to view the preaching of women as an ordinary practice within the life of the church. Each woman's claim to possess an extraordinary call to proclaim the gospel was judged on its own merits. Just as in the case of his lay preachers, so also Wesley evaluated a woman's calling on the basis of gifts, grace, and fruits. Moreover, Wesley maintained strict control over the activities of aspiring women preachers. If matters ever got out of hand, he acted swiftly to reestablish equilibrium. "I desire Mr. Peacock to put a final stop to the preaching of women in his circuit," he wrote forcefully to George Robinson in 1780. "If it were suffered, it would grow, and we know not where it would end."[6]

In this situation Wesley was responding to a specific set of circumstances. What appears to be a clear prohibition is, in reality, a reaffirmation of Wesley's basic conception of an extraordinary ministry—one manifestation of the exceptional nature of the Methodist movement. He could never allow the exceptional to become a general rule. This was a basic principle of Wesley's churchmanship. He realized that he was walking a tightrope, and he was content to live within the context of the dangers. But how could he admit the Crosbys and the Bosanquets to his circle of colleagues and prohibit the ministry of other "extraordinary messengers" who happened to be women? He continued to struggle with this issue. The extraordinary cases, however, appeared to be far less isolated than Wesley ever imagined. Throughout the course of the decade, the number of women preachers quickly increased. They exerted their influence throughout the British Isles. The floodgates were open.

## An Ever-widening Circle

About the same time that Wesley was conferring with the Cross Hall women about their work, Ann Gilbert began preaching in her native Cornwall. "One blessed fruit of the work which God had wrought in me," she confided to her journal, "was a more than usual concern for the salvation of poor sinners."[7] When she was asked to address a meeting of the young people, she says that she "was so filled with the peace and love of God, that I could not but exhort and intreat them to repent." Soon after, she consulted Wesley on the subject of her speaking in public. After listening to her testimony, Wesley is reported to have said, in characteristically terse fashion: "Sister, do all the good you can."

Zechariah Taft relates an interesting anecdote from her ministry in Cornwall:

> I have been informed that however opposed to women's preaching the preachers were who were appointed to that circuit, they were soon convinced that Ann Gilbert was eminently holy and useful. But on one occasion a person informed her that the new preacher had given it out that he would silence her. . . . Her answering on hearing this was "if Mr. —, can produce more converts than I, I will give it up."[8]

Wesley's itinerant, soon convinced of Ann's calling, wisely backed off. In fact, he assisted in opening the Methodist chapels of western Cornwall to her ministry.

In a letter to Mary Barritt, one of Wesley's "sons in the gospel" offers this unique eyewitness account of her preaching: "I had the pleasure of hearing Mrs. Ann Gilbert preach in the Chapel at Redruth, to about 1400 people. She had a torrent of softening eloquence, which occasioned a general weeping through the whole congregation. And what was more astonishing she was almost blind, and had been so for many years."[9]

In Ireland, Eliza Bennis continued to advise Wesley concerning developments there. And these were exciting days for Irish Methodism. During this period of tremendous religious renewal, Margaret Davidson emerged as Ireland's first woman preacher. She had overcome monumental obstacles in her pilgrimage of faith. Her blindness and disfigurement became the marks of responsible discipleship in a broken world. On May 1, 1765, she heard Wesley preach at a service in Newtownards. The experience, and her encounter with Wesley, would shape the rest of her life. "After preaching," she recalls, "he took me gently by the hand and said, 'Faint not, go on, and you shall see in glory!' These words left a lasting impression on my mind."[10]

It was in Lisburn that she began to exercise the unusual gifts that she possessed. She visited among her neighbors, prayed with them, and occasionally assisted at public services. Timid and unassuming by nature, she wished to avoid giving any possible offense. She was careful, as she says, never to "presume to stand up as an exhorter, lest any should take an occasion to say that I assumed the character of a preacher, which might have hurt the cause of God."[11] During the winter of 1769–70, however, she found herself caught up in the great revival that took place at Ballinderry. And again, in 1776, she ignited a spiritual flame that swept through the community of Ballyculter.

In that same year, Margaret met the Reverend and Mrs. Smyth at Derryaghy. At a meeting in Dunsford, at the insistence of the Reverend Smyth, she addressed the assembly. The effects of her clear intellect and retentive memory, her great fluency and fervor of speech, and the simplicity of her witness were immediate. Smyth advised her to stay and work among the people. Regular evening meetings were arranged, and many flocked to hear the effective preaching of this blind messenger from God. Within a month no fewer than one hundred persons had experienced a powerful spiritual awakening in their lives.

According to Margaret, her general approach in preaching was to draw out the themes of Scripture, primarily through the Wesleyan hymns that were so popular. Before she left, Margaret established new classes, bands, and Societies throughout the district. She was inundated with invitations to preach and to pioneer the development of Methodist Societies elsewhere. In spite of her blindness, she managed to itinerate at least a few weeks each year to the end of her life.

Elizabeth Hurrell joined the tight circle of women preachers in Yorkshire sometime during the early 1770s. Preaching with Wesley's approval, Elizabeth followed an itinerary that carried her throughout the northern counties of Yorkshire, Lancashire, and Derbyshire. Her ministry was soon in great demand. In a letter to Sarah Crosby, she reveals something of her industrious schedule:

> I arrived with God's blessing on Saturday week, where I have full employ, and here I believe it is the Lord's will I should be for a season; but rest now satisfied, and wait the Lord's direction.
>
> If nothing prevent, I intend going from hence to Sheffield, Doncaster, York, and stop a little at Pocklington, Beverley, Driffield, and from thence to Scarborough, and then where the Lord pleases to appoint.[12]

Zechariah Taft claims that her preaching "often manifested such a strength of thought, and felicity of expression, as were irresistibly impressive."[13] Because of her amazing talents and the overwhelming response she often received, she posed a threat to many of her male colleagues. Her work, in fact, became the center of a heated controversy among Wesley's preachers in the north. It is clear from the debate that ensued that tensions were beginning to emerge over the question of women preachers once again. Elizabeth seems to have had a direct confrontation with Joseph Benson, Wesley's newly appointed Assistant in Newcastle and staunch antagonist to women preachers.

The draft of a virulent letter in Benson's handwriting illustrates the depth of feeling among some of the preachers on this volatile issue. The intended recipient was undoubtedly one of Wesley's itinerant preachers who was sympathetic to the cause of the women preachers, very probably Robert Empringham. "Passing over some things less material," writes Benson, "I hasten to assure you I am very sorry you should be so far overseen as to allow any female whatsoever to take your place in the pulpit." Such an action is contrary to "conscience," he maintains, for the apostle Paul demands "the absolute necessity of imposing silence on women in the congregation. Any transgression of this rule is inexcusable."

"It is a shame," he goes on to say, "'tis indecent, unbecoming the modesty of the sex for a woman to speak in the church. The actions of the women preachers place their very souls in peril!"

> Now dear friend, can you tell me why those who set aside this commandment of the Lord do not set aside all his other commandments? Can you tell me why those daring females, who seem to have stript themselves of the chief ornament of their sex, I mean chaste and humble modesty and made themselves naked to their shame do not also commit fornication, and adultery, get drunk and swear? . . . They have effrontery enough, to ascend a pulpit and harange a promiscuous congregation for an hour together, when they are by God himself expressly forbid to so much as speak (by way of teaching) in a public assembly.

Benson can discern no possible motivation in the women other than "pride, self-love, and a concern for their own honor." Why should the present age, he argues, be different from any other? "God raises up preachers of the superior sex to declare his gospel," so why allow those "who are seldom content with the station God has assigned them, but are ever usurping authority over the man" to disrupt God's order. Fearful of the worst, Benson concludes his harangue with a word of caution directed at the leadership of the Methodist movement:

> I wish Mr. Wesley and the brethren would take the matter into serious consideration. It is now high time to do it. If it is winked at for a few years, we shall have female preachers in abundance, more I dare say than men . . . till behold the sexes have changed places, the woman is become the head of the man, the men almost all, learn in subjection and the women teach with authority! These things ought not so to be![14]

Benson was the mouthpiece for many who were frightened by the ever-widening sphere of women's activities within the life of the movement. Questions of authority, power, and status frequently shape the attitudes and actions of those in control. Personal animosities also find ready expression in the impersonal structures of an institution. Not only can the institution be used as an instrument of repression, it can also become a dangerous weapon in the hands of vindictive autocrats. Those wounds inflicted by members of the family, so to speak, were especially painful and hard for the women to bear.

But women preachers were always in peril, both from within and from without. On several occasions the mob pelted Madame Perrott with mud as she stood to preach. Her audiences were frequently tough and cruel. "Take up your cross; when the occasion offers, break through," Wesley admonishes Mary Bishop. "Speak, though it is pain and grief unto you."[15] Every time a woman preached, she placed herself in jeopardy. She knew that, and Wesley did too. He recognized the dangers, but he also saw the possibilities for building God's new order through these women. "I lament over every pious young woman," he exclaimed, "who is not as active as possible."[16] It was in the midst of persecution that he advised his faithful Assistant in Limerick, Eliza Bennis: "Up and be doing! Do not loiter. See that your talent rust not: rather let it gain ten more; and it will, if you use it."[17]

## "Women of Israel" in Yorkshire

Mary Bosanquet, Sarah Crosby, and Betsy Hurrell apparently never learned the meaning of the word *leisure*. Their talents never had an opportunity to rust. While the first recorded text of a woman preacher—"O Nebuchadnezzar, we are not careful to answer thee in this matter"—could easily be lost in its obscurity, Mary's preaching on that occasion was direct, powerful, and effective.[18] When Richard Waddy heard Mary preach at Bath he "felt power to give up his whole soul to God, in a way he never had done before."[19] Mary lost no opportunity of doing good. She was disciplined and responsive to God's call upon her life. But this did not mean that she was free from doubt, conflict, or anxiety.

On December 17, 1773, she confided to her journal: "Last Friday I went to Leeds to meet some classes. O how much do I suffer for every meeting I propose! The enemy follows me hard with such buffeting fears and discouragements as I cannot express. However, I determined to go, and leave the event to God."[20] At one point in her ministry, speaking in public created so much anxiety for her that she set apart a whole day in prayer to determine what she should do. Reflections from the day reveal the intensity of her anguish:

It cannot be expressed what I suffer:—it is only known to God what trials I go through in that respect. Lord, give me more humility, and then I shall not care for anything but thee! There are a variety of reasons why it is such a cross. The other day one told me, "He was sure I must be an impudent woman; no modest women, he was sure, could proceed thus!" Ah! how glad would nature be to find out,—Thou, Lord, dost not require it![21]

The fruit of her labor, however, was a continuous confirmation of her calling. In the midst of her intense struggle she was able to proclaim: "I had a clear conviction, God brought me to Yorkshire, and that I had a message to this people; and that notwithstanding the darkness which hung over my situation, I was at present where God would have me."[22] Accountable discipleship and mutual support from both brothers and sisters in the faith provided the reassurance she needed to continue on in her remarkable ministry.

One of the most significant days in Mary's life was September 17, 1776. On that day she preached to several thousand people at Goker and Huddersfield. Her vivid account of the experience is one of the most detailed portraits of a woman preacher in the Wesleyan revival:

Last Sabbath morning I went, according to appointment, to Goker. I arose early, and in pretty good health. The day was fine, though rather hot. About eleven we came to Huddersfield, and called on Mrs. H. She had asked me to lodge there on my return, and have a meeting, saying many had long desired it, and there would be no preaching there on that day. I felt immediately the people laid on my mind, and that I had a message to that place,—and said, "If the Lord permit, I will." She then said, "We will give it out at noon." We rode forward. Benjamin Cock met us, and kindly conducted us over the moors.

When we came to his hut, all was clean, and victuals enough provided for twenty men. But I was so heated with the ride, (nearly twenty miles,) and with the great fire on which they so liberally cooked for us, that I could not eat. My drinking nothing but water seemed also quite to distress them. They said the meeting had been given out in many places, and they believed we should have between two and three thousand people. That I did not believe; but there was indeed such a number, and of such a rabble as I scarce ever saw.

At one we went out to the rocks, a place so wild that I cannot describe it. The crowd which got around us was so great, that by striving which should get first to the quarry, (where we were to meet,) they rolled down great stones among the people below us, so that we feared mischief would be done. Blessed be God, none were hurt! I passed on among them on the top of the hill, not knowing whither I went. Twice I was pushed down by the crowd, but rose without being trampled on. We stopped on the edge of a spacious quarry filled with people, who were tolerably quiet. I gave out that hymn, *The Lord my pastures shall prepare, etc.* When they were a little settled, I found some liberty in speaking to them; and I believe most heard. As we returned into the house, numbers followed, and filled it so full we could not stir. I conversed with them, but could not get much answer. They stood like people in amaze, and seemed as if they could never have enough. Many wept and said, "When will you come again?"

We then set off for Huddersfield. I felt very much fatigued, and began to think, How shall I be able to fulfill my word there? As we rode along, brother Taylor said, "I think I ought to tell you my mind. I wish we could ride through Huddersfield, and not stop. For I know there are some there who do not like women to speak among them, and I fear you will meet with something disagreeable." I looked to the Lord, and received, as it seemed to me, the following direction: If I have a word to speak from him, he will make my way. If not, the door will be shut.

[When we arrived,] few of the principal persons had any objection, and the people much desired it; besides, as it had been given out at noon, there would be a great many strangers, whom it would not be well to disappoint. It was then agreed that we should have the meeting in the house, where they usually had the preaching; but when we came there the crowd was very great, and the place so hot, that I feared I should not be able to speak at all. I stood still, and left all to God. A friend gave out a hymn; during which some fainted away.

Brother Taylor said, "I perceive it is impossible for us to stay within doors, the people cannot bear the heat, and there are more without than are within." We then came out. My head swam with the heat; I scarce knew which way I went, but seemed carried along by the people, till we stopped at a horseblock, placed against a wall on the side of the street, with a plain wide opening before it. On the steps of this I stood, and gave out, "Come, ye sinners, poor and needy," etc.

While the people were singing the hymn, I felt a renewed conviction to speak in the name of the Lord. My bodily strength seemed to return each moment. I felt no weariness, and my voice was stronger than in the morning, while I was led to enlarge on these words, "The Lord is our Judge, the Lord is our Lawgiver, the Lord is our King, he will save us." . . . Deep solemnity sat on every face. I think there was scarce a cough to be heard, or the least motion; though the number gathered was very great. So solemn a time I have seldom known; my voice was clear enough to reach them all; and when we concluded I felt stronger than when we began.[23]

Many of Mary's friends advised her to assume the status of a traveling preacher. She did not believe, however, that this was her calling. Others suggested that she become a woman preacher among the Quakers. But Mary loved the Methodists and had long since decided to "stick to them like a leech," regardless of the consequences. Her response to Methodist critics was swift and clear. "I do nothing," she would retort, "but what Mr. Wesley approves; and as to reproach thrown by some on me, what have I to do with it, but quietly go forward, saying, 'I will be still more vile,' if my Lord requires it!"[24]

At this same time Sarah Crosby began a virtual whirlwind campaign across the trackless Yorkshire moors and dales. And thus began a legacy of lengthy journeys that would continue for some twenty years. It was not uncommon for her to hold as many as four meetings a day, addressing as many as five hundred persons who had eagerly gathered to hear her preach. Her journal offers us a glimpse of a typical day:

I spent an hour at five, with as many as could come,— had a very solemn meeting at the preaching house, at half past eight; I believed it would be a good time, and so it was. The people came from many places round about. By one o'clock, four or five hundred were gathered together, with whom I had a very solemn time, and much of the presence of God. I met the class at five, and another public meeting at seven,—there were more present than before. I am astonished at the strength of body my Lord gives me; I ascribe it all to him.[25]

Sarah often accompanied Wesley on his journeys through the northern counties. Leaving her "dear Father in the Gospel" at Scarborough, she ventured out on her own on a three-week campaign that took her to Guisborough, Newton, Stokesley, Potto, Bransdale, Highton-Dale, Gillamore, Lastingham, Bilsdale, and Northallerton. At every stop, anxious villagers anticipated her visits. In her journal, Mary Holder recalls the excitement created by her arrival:

After some months Mrs. Crosby came again to Scarborough, and Miss Hurrel came with her; and they were the means of many flocking to the house of God. Their labours publicly and privately were blest in town and country to numbers of precious souls. Mrs. Crosby, continued to come to Whitby several times for some years. She stayed with us in my father's house many weeks, and was a pattern of holiness in all manner of conversation. Her life and labours of love were of great use to many a soul, and I bless God that I ever saw her. . . . Her advice, reproof, instruction, and example were rendered exceedingly useful.[26]

Upon returning to her headquarters at Cross Hall in December 1774, her schedule hardly slackened, even through the bitter winter months. At Bradford, a crowd consisting of "quakers, baptists, church folks, and methodists" was so great that they feared the collapse of the meeting house galleries. Sarah was humbled by the experience:

On Sunday evening while I was standing up in the great preaching house, surrounded by upwards of two thousand souls, my good Lord, who never leaves those who trust in him, brought to my remembrance the time wherein he shewed me, that if I could talk to as many souls as could possibly hear me to the end of my life, it would be but a little handful compared with what the whole world contained.[27]

In the midst of these labors, having preached in chapels, houses, barns, and open fields, in summer heat and winter chill, Sarah says: "I was as sure that I was employed by my Lord and doing his will, as of my own life." On the last day of 1777, she summarized her round of activities for the year:

> Thou hast enabled me, from the first of last January to the fourth of this month (December), to ride 960 miles, to keep 220 public meetings, at many of which some hundreds of precious souls were present, about 600 private meetings, and to write 116 letters, many of them long ones; besides many, many conversations with souls in private, the effect of which will, I trust, be "as bread cast on the waters." All glory be unto him, who has strengthened his poor worm.[28]

Sarah Crosby's success and influence is unquestionable. The impressions she left on the minds of her hearers were deep. Frances Mortimer heard her preach on December 1, 1774: "Mrs. Crosby expounded the 13th chapter of the first epistle to the Corinthians. She explained the characters of divine charity, or love, with a simplicity I had never heard before. Her heart and words acted in concert. Every sentence was impressive, and carried conviction to the heart. . . . My soul panted for that love on which she so delightfully expatiated."[29] Her reputation as one of the most gifted preachers of the time preceded her wherever she went.

To another aspiring woman preacher she described the essential relationship between her personal experience of God's love and her calling to proclaim it to others:

I hope My Dear Friend will be glad to hear, that our Lord
continues to pour out His Spirit amongst us. . . . And what
is astonishing even to ourselves is, that our Lord is doing
this great work, by the most simple means.

As for myself, my Dear, I know not what to say, but that,
the immeasurable comfort swells my own transported
breast! For he reneweth my strength as the eagle. I live in a
holy astonishment before my God, while He fills my soul
with divine power, and the simplicity of a little child, and
never was so continually filled, yea overflowed with love
before. Indeed my Lord shews me the reason was because I
hearkened too much to the voice which said, hold thy
peace; keep thy happiness to thyself. (Tho' not enough to
please them neither.) But He now forbids me, to hide, the
Light He gives, under a bushel. And the more simply I witness for God, the more does He witness in my heart, and
others too, Glory be to His dear name forever. "O let my
mouth be fill'd with thy praise, while, all the day long I
publish thy grace."[30]

Despite widespread prejudice against women preachers,
Sarah was more convinced than ever that she must
improve her talent: "I had a very good time, and a house
full of people. In the evening I went up to the top of the
hill, and was so sensible when praying alone, that I was
doing my master's blessed will, in going among the people
that no outward voice could have strengthened the conviction. My spirit rests herein—In the arms of divine love."[31]

The work of these "women of Israel" in Yorkshire was
admired and sanctioned by many of the leaders of the
Wesleyan revival. John Pawson, one of Wesley's most
respected preachers in Leeds, opened doors for many of
the women in the communities he served. He offered the
use of the preaching house in Leeds to Sarah whenever she
desired it. The Reverend John Fletcher, Wesley's designated successor, was one of the strongest advocates for the
women. His words to Mary Bosanquet express the sentiment of many who rejoiced over the extraordinary work of
these extraordinary women:

My Christian love waits upon Mrs. Crosby, Miss Hurrel, and Miss Ritchie. I hope the Lord binds you each day closer to Himself and to each other, and enables you to see and experience the glory of the promise made to the daughters and handmaids, as well as to the sons and servants of the Lord. Oh, what a day when we shall all be so filled with power from on high, as to go forth and prophesy, and water the Lord's drooping plants and barren parched garden with rivers of living water flowing from our own souls.[32]

# Chapter 7

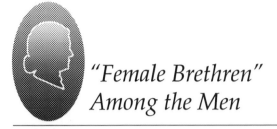

## *"Female Brethren" Among the Men*

The ministry of the women preachers blossomed during the final decade of Wesley's life. Women raised their voices to proclaim the gospel from Cornwall to the North Yorkshire moors, from the industrial cities of the north to the idyllic villages of the west. Because of Wesley's influence, the Methodist Conference in England was gradually led to authorize the work of these exceptional women.

### Recognizing the Labor and the Fruit

One historian of Cornish Methodism correctly observes that women preachers were all but unknown in that region of England. Elizabeth Tonkin, however, is one shining exception. She followed directly in the footsteps of her friend and mentor, Ann Gilbert. Ann had already gained something of a reputation as a preacher at Gwinear when she befriended this impressionable sixteen-year-old. Her preaching shaped Elizabeth's faith. Her life of devotion modeled a way of spiritual formation that was balanced and joyful. Ann became Elizabeth's spiritual guide and homiletical tutor.

Elizabeth's preaching began on the eve of her twentieth birthday in 1782. She had just moved to the village of

Feock. Her son later described the circumstances of Elizabeth's calling in a manuscript account of her life:

> One Sunday evening the preacher appointed for Feock
> was prevented from attending, by the recent death of his
> daughter, and no other was sent to supply his place. . . .
> Some called on my mother to speak to them, which she at
> first refused to do, saying she had never so engaged in her
> life. However, she at last consented to give out a hymn, and
> pray with them, hoping this would satisfy them; and when
> she had done this; she strove to dismiss them, but the
> attempt was vain; they still persisted in their request, and
> told her plainly if she did not speak to them they would not
> go away for the night.[1]

Elizabeth gave in, and, as she says, "the power of God came down among them." Her congregation announced that she would preach again the following Sunday. And thus she was propelled into a new phase in her life. When Joseph Taylor, the superintending minister in the circuit, was apprised of her "irregular activities," he simply chose to overlook them. When he had an opportunity to meet the aspiring preacher, the Reverend Taylor is said to have greeted her warmly, saying: "Well Betsy, I did not open your mouth, and I will not shut it." The influence of her ministry was soon felt throughout Cornwall.

Her marriage to a Mr. Collett in 1785 never slackened her pace. "For nearly twenty years," her son, Richard, recalls, "she frequently held meetings in the neighbouring places on the Lord's-day, and sometimes on the working-day evenings also." She combined the work of a mother and homemaker with that of a preacher with uncommon skill. This mother of eleven, and faithful partner in a marriage of some forty years, found new avenues of ministry in every community she made her home.

In the nineteenth century, Elizabeth's story was suppressed. When Richard Collett's account of her life was sent to Jabez Bunting, editor of the widely circulated

*Methodist Magazine,* he refused to print it. He feared that it would "be a precedent to young females in the connexion, who are ready to step into the work."[2] Likewise, a moving account of her life and experience which did appear in that publication was incorrectly attributed to "Mr." rather than "Mrs." E. C. These were insignificant matters, however, for one who was "ever ready out of the good treasure of her heart to bring forth good things."

While Elizabeth seems to have conducted her ministry somewhat single-handedly, other women combined their efforts after the model of the Cross Hall community. When Wesley's itinerary took him through the counties of Norfolk and Suffolk in the fall of 1781, he made a remarkable discovery:

> *Mon. 29*—I went to Fakenham, and in the evening preached in the room built by Miss Franklin, now Mrs. Parker. I believe most of the town were present.
> *Tues. 30*—I went to Wells, . . . where also Miss Franklin had opened a door, by preaching abroad, though at the peril of her life. She was followed by a young woman of the town, with whom I talked largely, and found her very sensible, and much devoted to God. From her I learnt that, till the Methodists came, they had none but female teachers in this country; and that there were six of these within ten or twelve miles, all of whom were members of the Church of England.[3]

Wesley was very much impressed with their work. There is no question that this event swept away any remaining prejudice in Wesley's mind. These women were doing the work of God. And whether they exerted a direct influence upon their Methodist sisters, or vice versa, was inconsequential to Wesley. He was excited, however, to discover a number of women in his Norwich Circuit who had, themselves, taken up the work. Standing in the vanguard was a young woman named Mary Sewell.

Little is known about Mary's early life in the small village of Thurlton. William Lamb may have been present at the inception of her ministry when he "heard a Miss Sewell give an exhortation in a small home in the village."[4] She removed many of Adam Clarke's prejudices when he visited the circuit in 1784. On April 28, he had the opportunity to hear Mary preach on the classic Wesleyan text, Ephesians 2:8. He left this remarkable account of her proclamation of God's saving grace:

> I have this morning heard Miss Sewell preach; she has a good talent for exhortation, and her words spring from a heart that evidently feels deep concern for the souls of the people; and, consequently, her hearers are interested and affected. I have formerly been no friend to female preaching; but my sentiments are a little altered. If God give to a holy woman, a gift for exhortation and reproof, I see no reason why it should not be used. This woman's preaching has done much good; and fruits of it may be found copiously, in different places in the circuit.[5]

These were high words of commendation from one of the greatest scholars of the early Methodist movement.

Mary risked her life on at least one occasion when she faced the mob at Yarmouth and testified to her faith. But she was welcomed with open arms in many of the villages throughout Norfolk and Suffolk. The oldest register that has been preserved from Yarmouth, which then formed part of the Norwich Circuit, contains the names of the Methodist preachers of 1785. It is noteworthy that on the second page of the record, we find "Sister Mary Sewell" included among the names of the "local preachers."[6]

Mary was not alone in her work. Adam Clarke had the opportunity to hear one of her colleagues, Mrs. Proudfoot, shortly after meeting her. His brief paragraph recalling her reflections on Exodus 3:3 is the only record of her life and labors. It provides but a meager glimpse into the world of this spiritual pioneer:

> She spoke several pertinent things, which tended both to conviction and consolation; and seems to possess genuine

piety. If the Lord choose to work in this way, shall my eye be evil because He is good? God forbid! Rather let me extol that God, who, by . . . preaching, saves those who believe in Jesus. Thou, Lord, choosest to confound the wisdom of the world by foolishness, and its strength by weakness, that no soul may glory in thy presence; and that the excellency of the power may be seen to belong to Thee, alone. Had not this been the case, surely I had never been raised up to call sinners to repentance.[7]

A number of Wesley's less favorably disposed itinerants launched an attack upon the women preachers at the momentous Conference convened at Leeds in 1784. Wesley defended the women's activities on the basis of their "extraordinary call." One old veteran, Thomas Mitchell, went one step further and reminded his colleagues of a somewhat embarrassing point. "I know not what you would do with the good women," he instructed their opponents, "for all the fish they catch they put into our net."[8]

## A Formal Act

One of the most celebrated women preachers of the day was Sarah Mallet. Wesley was always intrigued by spiritual phenomena, and he was captivated by Sarah's story:

I found her in the very house to which I went, and went and talked with her at large. . . . Of the following relation, which she gave me, there are numberless witnesses.
Some years since it was strongly impressed upon her that she ought to call sinners to repentance. This impression she vehemently resisted, believing herself quite unqualified, both by her sin and her ignorance, till it was suggested, "If you do it not willingly, you shall do it whether you will or no." She fell into a fit, and, while utterly senseless, thought she was in the preaching-house on Lowestoft, where she prayed and preached for near an hour, to a numerous congregation. She then opened her eyes, and recovered her senses. In a year or two she had

eighteen of these fits, in every one of which she imagined herself to be preaching in one or another congregation. She then cried out, "Lord, I *will* obey Thee; I *will* call sinners to repentance." She has done so occasionally from that time; and her fits returned no more.[9]

There is no question that Sarah had come under the influence of Mary Sewell, who preached frequently in the villages of Sarah's youth. In her own words, Sarah describes the inward call to preach she experienced and her initial resistance to it:

It was imprest on my mind, to speak in public for God: and those words were continually before me, Reprove, rebuke, exhort! Nor could I by any means drive them out of my thoughts. But I could not bear the thought, having been in time past no friend of women's preaching. I therefore resolved never to do any such thing, be the consequence what it would. From that moment it seemed as if the powers of darkness overwhelmed my soul: and I was forced to withdraw from the family, and pour out my soul before God.[10]

God's claim upon her life eventually triumphed, and Sarah began her remarkable public ministry in February 1786.

"These words," she writes, "had followed me for near a year, 'Ye shall be hated of all men for my name's sake': and so did those, 'Fear not; for I am with thee: be not afraid; for I am God.'" She spoke at her uncle's house every other Sunday evening. She experienced great peace. In her journal Sarah records the fact that, in the midst of these labors, "Mr. Wesley was to become a father and a faithful friend."[11] His encouragement was a continual source of strength. Moreover, his influence won for her the full support and authorization of the Manchester Conference of 1787. Sarah recalls the momentous event:

When I first travelled I followed Mr. Wesley's counsel, which was, to let the voice of the people be to me the voice of God;—and where I was sent for, to go, for the Lord had called me thither. To this counsel I have attended to this day. But the voice of the people was not the voice of some preachers. But Mr. Wesley soon made this easy by sending me a note from the Conference, by Mr. Joseph Harper, who was that year appointed for Norwich.[12]

This note is the single most important piece of documentary evidence concerning the women preachers of early Methodism. The official authorization simply reads: "We give the right hand of fellowship to Sarah Mallet, and have no objection to her being a preacher in our connexion, so long as she preaches the Methodist doctrines, and attends to our discipline."[13] Opposition did diminish as a consequence of this action. Sarah's ministry blossomed as she traveled throughout Norfolk and Suffolk in the tradition of her sister preachers.

In no sense was Sarah anything less than a Wesleyan traveling preacher:

> My way of preaching from the first is to take a text and divide it, and speak from the different heads. For many years when we had but few Chapels in this Country, I preached in the open air and in barns—and in waggons. After I was married I was with my husband in the preachers plan, for many years. He was a Local Preacher thirty-two years, and finished his work and his life well.
>
> I am glad some of our preachers see it right to encourage female preaching. I hope they will all, both Local and Travelling Preachers, think more on these words "quench not the Spirit," neither in themselves nor others. "Despise not prophesyings," no, not out of the mouth of a child,—then would they be more like Mr. Wesley: and I think more like Christ.[14]

Sarah's name was included in the schedule for preaching in the Circuit. Wesley conferred with her on matters of financial support for her ministry, books for her spiritual growth and formation, and protocol in her relationship with pastoral colleagues. When the question arose concerning the necessity of her being licensed as a nonconforming preacher, Wesley responded with a standard reply: "I do not require any of our preachers to license either themselves or the places where they preach."[15]

It would seem that Wesley's only concern was that Sarah might not be doing as much as she could. A letter of encouragement could sometimes carry the tone of a reprimand:

> I was a little surprised a while ago when one speaking of you said, "Sally Mallet is not so serious as Betty Reeve." I thought Sally Mallet was as serious as any young woman in Norfolk. Be wary in all your actions, and you will never want any assistance which is in the power of, my dear Sally,
>
> > Yours affectionately,
> > John Wesley[16]

Sarah continued—seriously—in a ministry of many years.

Elizabeth Reeve, whom Wesley mentions in this letter, was one of Sarah Mallet's converts. It was under her preaching that Elizabeth experienced a call to enter the ministry. When Wesley learned about her aspirations, he asked Sally to bring her to Diss so that he might talk with her about her experience. Convinced of her gifts and graces, Wesley encouraged her to proclaim the gospel and look for a good harvest. Writing to Sarah about her in 1790, Wesley observes: "It is well that you are acquainted with our sister that likewise is sometimes employed in the same labour of love; Providence has marked you out for friends to each other, and there should be no reserve between you. . . . If you go on in the work to which God has called you, you will experience trials upon trials."[17] Wesley recognized the importance of fellowship. And he knew that the women who were called to preach needed one another. He rejoiced at the discovery of such friendships.

He followed the progress of these sister preachers with affectionate interest. On December 15, 1789, he offered the following advice to Sarah concerning her preaching and leadership in worship:

> It gives me pleasure to hear that prejudice dies away and our preachers behave in a friendly manner. What is now more wanting in order to recover your health you yourself plainly see. Be not at every one's call. This you may quite cut off by going nowhere without the advice of Mr. Tattershall. Never continue the service above an hour at once, singing, *preaching,* prayer, and all. You are not to judge by your own *feelings,* but by the word of God. Never scream. Never speak above the natural pitch of your voice; it is disgustful to the hearers. It gives them pain, not pleasure. And it is destroying yourself. It is offering God murder for sacrifice. Only follow these three advices, and you will have a larger share in the regard of, my dear Sally, Yours affectionately, John Wesley.[18]

## "Female Brethren" and Colleagues

When Robert Roe heard Mary Bosanquet preach at Leeds, he was overwhelmed by the power of her words. "So much wisdom, dignity, and piety, joined to so much childlike simplicity," he observes, "I never saw before."[19] Mary was a veteran preacher. June 8, 1781, marked thirteen years of ministry in the Cross Hall community of Yorkshire. The next day, Mary received a letter that would propel her into one of the most remarkable romances of early Methodism. The Reverend John Fletcher, Wesley's most trusted friend and designated successor, spoke to Mary of his growing admiration and secret affection. In several months' time Mary sold her Yorkshire farm, settled all of the remaining orphans, and united in marriage with John on November 12, 1781.

The couple remained at Cross Hall until January 2, 1782, when they set out for Madeley where John served as pastor in the local Anglican Church. "Mr. Fletcher stole hallowed fire from my people," John Valton confided to his journal, "by taking away Miss Bosanquet to Madeley."[20]

Yorkshire's loss was Madeley's gain. On the first Sunday of their return to John's church, he introduced his new wife and boldly proclaimed: "I have not married this wife for myself only, but for your sakes also."[21] John and Mary formed a unique partnership of mutual service and love, perhaps the first "clergy couple," so to speak, within the Methodist movement. They functioned as co-pastors, for all practical purposes, throughout the course of their marriage.

The people of Madeley were extremely receptive to Mary's ministry. "My call is also so clear," she was soon able to affirm, "and I have such liberty in the work, and such sweet encouragement among the people."[22] Mary contributed greatly to the cultivation of a vital faith among her new neighbors. Her reputation spread rapidly throughout the community. William Tranter describes her activities in some detail:

> Tribes were seen going up from all the neighbouring places early on the Sabbath morning, for Mrs. Fletcher's nine o-clock meeting, full of joy, or of joyous expectation of having gracious manifestations from their Lord.
>
> On a week-day evening service, it was not unusual to see the room crowded with attentive and delighted hearers, while this blessed woman was expounding, generally, some historic portion of Scripture. . . . The effect produced was often truly astonishing.
>
> It was not uncommon to see two, three, or more Clergymen, pious and able men, from neighbouring and even distant parishes, among the congregation at these evening lectures.[23]

This wonderful romance and shared ministry was cut short by John's tragic death in 1785. They enjoyed only four brief years of life in ministry together. Mary was crushed. "My loss is beyond the power of words to paint. I have gone through deep waters but nothing to this. Well I want no pleasant prospect but upward, nor anything whereon to fix my hope but immortality. . . . The sun of my

earthly joys is set forever."[24] Mary's sense of John's continued presence with her sustained her through this dark
hour. The pain of grief was soon transformed into renewed
dedication to God and to the mission Mary shared with
her "most sympathizing and heavenly friend." "I found
the dear children which my beloved Partner had left
behind, laid upon my mind," she confides to her journal.
"I saw I must act among them, and meet the people the
same as before."

And so during the years following her husband's death,
Mary not only continued her regular preaching services at
Madeley, but expanded her ministry throughout the area.
Fired by a profound sense of Christian vocation, Mary
became a living example of the richness and abundance of
life offered to us in Christ. Her own words are a living testimony to the depth of her spirit and the breadth of her
influence:

> The same Lord that opened my mouth, and endued me
> with power, and gave me courage to speak His Word, has
> through His grace enabled me to continue to the present
> day. The Lord has been, and is now the comfort and sup-
> port of my soul in all trials. And, thank God, I have not run
> in vain, neither laboured in vain. There are some witnesses
> in heaven and some on earth.[25]

It is not surprising that Mary functioned as a prototype
for many Methodist women. They were attracted by her
magnetism and modeled their own ministries upon her
dynamic life and work. Sarah Lawrence, Mary's constant
companion throughout the course of her life, is but one
example. Mary's "beloved Sally," the orphaned niece of
Sarah Ryan, was more like a daughter than a devoted servant. Mary carefully nurtured the unique gifts she saw in
her little friend. In 1778 she secretly expressed hopes that
Sally would follow in her own footsteps: "A visible concern arose in her mind, more forsible than ever, for the
souls of the people and in particular of the rising genera-

tion. And such a gift was then given her for children, as I have hardly seen in any one, and a love like that of a parent."[26]

Sarah succumbed to the contagious effects of Mary's love. Her life did duplicate Mary's in many ways as she sought to express that same loving spirit in all that she did. At Madeley, Sarah began meetings in one of the most depressed areas within the parish. She visited from door to door. Her life was characterized by that unique balance of personal piety and social service that was a hallmark of Leytonstone/Cross Hall heritage. Her evangelism was life-centered. Mary described the expansion of her ministry and the development of her style: "She began meetings in different places, on which numbers attended. Her method was, after singing and prayer, to read some life, experience, or some awakening author, stopping now and then, to explain and apply it as the Lord gave her utterance. And several, who are now lively believers in our connexion, were brought in through that means."[27]

She preached every other Sunday evening for four years in the small village of Coalport. She loved the miners and their families; and her preaching expressed the depth of her feelings for that community: "If ever I was called any where, I surely was to that place. It seemed at times, as if my whole soul were drawn out in their behalf; and, when I think of the dear children, and grown persons too, who used to come through such deep roads to meet me, I cannot help turning my eyes, with tears and prayers, many times towards that spot."[28]

When Mary Fletcher moved to Madeley, the remaining women preachers of the Cross Hall community moved to Leeds. They took up residence in a small house adjacent to the old Methodist chapel there, a home known locally as the old Boggard House. Sarah Crosby and Ann Tripp assumed leadership of a strong and influential band of women preachers who styled themselves—with unconscious humor—as "The Female Brethren."[29] Elizabeth Hurrell and Sarah Stevens certainly participated in the ongoing life of this circle. And in later years, Mary Barritt, one of the greatest evangelists of the early nineteenth century, played some part as well.

The ranks of "female brethren" swelled throughout the course of the 1780s. A new generation of women preachers was emerging on the scene. A new group of women with a dynamic vision of their place within the Methodist movement carried the mantle forward. The past was reborn. In a letter to Ellen Gretton, pioneer of Methodism in Grantham and preacher throughout Wesley's native county of Lincoln, the aged apostle of Methodism makes one final reference to the originative events of the Epworth rectory:

> In the new sphere of action to which Providence has called you, I trust you will find new zeal for God and new vigour in pursuing every measure which may tend to the furtherance of His kingdom. In one of my mother's letters you may observe something resembling your case. She began only with permitting two or three of her neighbours to come to the family prayers on Sunday evening. But they increased to an hundred, yea above an hundred and fifty. Go humbly and steadily on, consulting the Assistant in all points, and pressing on to perfection.[30]

Alice Cambridge, of Bandon, Ireland, typifies the female preacher of the turn of the century. Frustrated by opposition from some of the Irish Methodist leaders, she sought Wesley's advice. His reply, written only a month prior to his death, stands as a dying testimony to the transforming power of God's love and the eternal significance of conscience in response to God's call—both legacies from his mother:

> I received your letter an hour ago. I thank you for writing so largely and so freely; do so always to me as your friend, as one that loves you well. Mr. Barber has the glory of God at heart; and so have his fellow labourers. Give them all honour, and obey them in all things as far as con-

science permits. But it will not permit you to be silent when God commands you to speak: yet I would have you give as little offence as possible; and therefore I would advise you not to speak at any place where a preacher is speaking at the same time, lest you should draw away his hearers. Also avoid the first appearance of pride or magnifying yourself. If you want books or anything, let me know; I have your happiness much at heart.[31]

Alice was remarkably neat, plain, and Quaker-like in appearance. She was a stout woman with a pleasant accent and extraordinary powers of speech. The predominant theme of her preaching was the goodness of God. This, she gratefully acknowledged, was the source of her peace and life. She was modest in manner, but indomitable with regard to her call. In the years following Wesley's death, she became so successful that her work was a perennial source of embarrassment to her male colleagues. They became increasingly antagonistic, and their opposition to "female preaching" soon exploded into a raging debate.

During the 1780s great strides were made within Methodism toward a fuller realization of a ministry for women. The official authorization of Sarah Mallet by the Conference in 1787 was a monumental step climaxing a lengthy process of change. Mary Fletcher, Elizabeth Tonkin, the preachers of Norfolk and Suffolk, and the "Female Brethren" of Leeds all received widespread support for their remarkable ministries. But there was a storm gathering momentum. The suspense began to build as one of the women's greatest advocates, John Wesley, came closer and closer to death.

The women had come too far, however, to be deterred now by the threat of a storm. Come what may, they were determined to give their all for God. Their story was forged on the crucible of struggle and pain. On June 20, 1790, the first woman preacher of Methodism, Sarah Crosby, encouraged a sister in Christ who was aspiring to preach. She describes the central conviction that sustained her life and ministry, and the witness and service of all devoted followers of the Christ:

> When we know we have our Lord's approbation, we should stand, like the beaten anvil to the stroke; or lie in his hands, as clay in the hands of the potter. Through evil report, and good, we pass, but all things worketh together for good, to them that love God. Speak and act, as the spirit gives liberty, and utterance; fear not the face of man, but with humble confidence, trust in the Lord; looking unto him who is able, and willing to save to the uttermost, all that come unto God by him.[32]

# Chapter 8

 *The Controversy Explodes*

John Wesley died on the morning of Wednesday, March 2, 1791. He was eighty-seven. It is not surprising that the event of Wesley's death created a crisis within the Methodist Connection. While he had made preparations for the future of the Methodist movement, the founder had become so closely identified with the revival that it was difficult to conceive of Methodism apart from Wesley. Dissension arose within the Methodist ranks. Alexander Kilham seceded from the Wesleyans to establish the New Connexion in 1797. This was but the first of a number of schisms. The whole movement stood at the most critical juncture of its history.

In addition to these internal issues, certain external factors contributed to the crisis. The French Revolution greatly affected the political outlook of the English people. It stiffened their conservatism and decreased their level of tolerance. On the domestic scene, radical social changes brought about by the industrial revolution created a sense of instability and uncertainty. That wave of change, which had gathered momentum throughout the course of the century, had now arched itself into a thunderous mass. It was about to crash as the old world gave way to "modern" life.

The ancient world groaned under the pain of new birth.

How was the church to respond to the needs of an age in radical transition? What models and forms should the church adopt in its effort to be faithful to the gospel as it moved with society into a new era? It is during this volatile period that the women preachers of Methodism approached their zenith. At the same time, however, the question of women's preaching became one of the most bitterly contested controversies in the life of the church. Subsequent developments, while never inevitable, were certainly predictable. In little more than a decade following Wesley's death, harsh restrictions were placed upon the activity of women preachers. In some quarters the preaching of women was formally forbidden.

## Entering a New Era

During the revivalistic period immediately following Wesley's death there were many women who openly exercised their gifts in the ministry of preaching. The first generation of women preachers, including Mary Fletcher and Sarah Crosby, began to recede into the background as a new breed of women took their place. The wives of Wesleyan itinerants frequently exhorted, prophesied, and preached with their husbands in the Methodist circuits. Many of the women carried on their labors as a living testimony to their "reverend father," Mr. Wesley. The aging Sarah Crosby encouraged an aspiring preacher by echoing Wesley's words to her: "Our reverend and dear Father's direction to me used to be, 'Do all you can for God.' I believe it would be the same to you, because Moses like Mr. Wesley, would say, 'Oh, that all the Lord's people were Prophets.'"[1]

An abundance of new names floods the records of the growing Methodist Societies—women who struggled with God's call to preach the Word. Mary Woodhouse Holder, Mary Wiltshaw, Sarah Stevens, Sarah Cox, Sarah Eland. New names, new excitement, but the same conviction of heart and spirit: God called them to offer Christ to the people of their time, and nothing was going to deter them. Sarah Eland makes that clear in her journal: "Ah! had they known the inward travail of my soul, and the great aversion I always felt to publicity; they must have concluded it to have been no ordinary operation of the Spirit. . . . I am as certain as to my call from God to speak in his name, as I was clear in a sense of his pardoning mercy, through Christ my Saviour."[2]

At Nottingham, Sarah preached to some two thousand persons. Mary Harrison preached every Sunday evening at neighboring Wishall. Margaret Watson awakened the slumbering Society at Redcar with her regular preaching in the Methodist chapel. Hannah Parker of Ampleforth preached in barns and in the open air throughout North Riding of Yorkshire. The "Service Register" for Houghton-Le-Spring near Sunderland reveals that Mary Goulden preached at Wapping. Her text from 2 Thessalonians concerning judgment, flaming fire, and the punishment of eternal destruction reveals something of the new revivalistic fervor.

In Bingley, Elizabeth Dickinson created considerable excitement when she preached in the open air. Her experience had been similar to that of Sarah Mallet. Thousands flocked to hear her, and many professed their conversions through her instrumentality. Her oratory was moving. Her powers of persuasion were matchless. And her preaching maintained that essential Wesleyan balance of faith working by love. One eyewitness testifies to the nature of her ministry: "Her motto was holiness to the Lord. She has often said we must not only preach the gospel, but live the gospel, or we shall do more harm than good. . . . I have heard her give out hymns, sing, and pray, and exhort the people to flee from the wrath to come, in such a pathetic manner, that I have seen tears like showers, flow from the eyes of crowded audiences."[3]

These women were discovering something "primitive"

in the faith. Their fervor and zeal were alien to the ordered spirituality of the emerging Wesleyan Methodist Church. The style of this new generation of women evangelists precluded their acceptance among the respectable leaders of the Methodist hierarchy.

## The Storm-center: Mary Barritt

In his later years, Wesley preferred to believe that prejudice against women preachers was declining among his Societies. In this confidence, however, he was mistaken. In the decade following his death, hardening antifeminist sentiment focused increasingly upon the ministry of one woman in particular: Mary Barritt. She was unquestionably the most famous female evangelist of the early nineteenth century. In 1827 she published an extensive account of her work as a revivalist. This autobiography demonstrates her preeminence as an itinerant preacher of unparalleled ability and success.[4]

Mary was born at Hay in 1772. After joining the Methodist Society at neighboring Colne (Lancashire) she followed the typical pattern of her fellow-laborers in the gospel. Prayer in class meetings, and testimony and exhortation at the love-feasts, soon led to preaching. Her actions aroused immediate hostility. Lancelot Harrison, the itinerant appointed to her circuit was vehemently opposed to women preachers, and he let his feeling be known. "All that I have suffered from the world in the way of reproach and slander," grieved Mary, "is little in comparison with what I have suffered from some professors of religion, as well as even ministers of the gospel."[5]

Her supporters rallied, however, when her spirits drooped. "It is at the peril of your soul," William Sagar warned the antagonist Harrison, "that you meddle with Mary Barritt: God is with her—fruit is appearing wherever she goes."[6] Some of the most prominent leaders within Methodism—John Pawson, Alexander Mather, Thomas

Vasey, Samuel Bradburn, William Bramwell, Thomas Shaw, and many others—counted Mary a close friend and frequently invited her to preach in their pulpits. In 1794 she began a series of preaching pilgrimages that continued for many years. During one of her prolonged campaigns in the Nottingham Circuit, no fewer than five hundred members were added to that Society in one quarter.

Unprecedented growth always followed in the wake of her preaching:

> In the Yorkshire Dales, extending from Ripon to Bainbridge, Reeth, and Richmond, the Lord enabled me, and others, to gather the harvest, in handfuls, and everywhere he gave us fruit, for, at that time, those circuits had little help from the travelling preachers. . . . Suffice it to say, that the Almighty, in a most extraordinary manner, removed my scruples, answered my objections, and thrust me out into his vineyard. Indeed, nothing but a powerful conviction that God required it at my hand . . . could have supported me in it.[7]

Mary's brand of evangelism was no mere revivalism. Like Wesley she provided meticulous care for her converts. She guided them into Methodist classes and saw to it that they were properly assimilated into the life of the Societies. Moreover, Mary's preaching was well balanced. On one occasion, Alexander Suter intimated that she proclaimed a shallow gospel based on one or two obscure texts. At the Quarterly Meeting held in Leeds, Edward Wade rose to her defense. He summarily dismissed these kinds of allegations. "I have now heard Miss Barritt, twenty-seven or twenty-eight times," he retorted, "and have never heard her speak twice from the same text." A close scrutiny of her records and accounts of her preaching reveal her wide-ranging knowledge and use of the Bible.

It is not surprising to find the names of some of the most prominent preachers of the day listed among her hundreds of converts—names such as Thomas Jackson, William

Dawson, Joseph Taylor, Thomas Garbutt, and Robert Newton. From these advocates, Mary received all the support and encouragement she needed to carry on her work. Letters of appreciation melted her despair in the face of mounting opposition:

> We approve of your preaching the gospel: we have come so to do, for God has blest your labours amongst us, and made you a lasting blessing to this day. We know that God has called you to preach his word, therefore, fear not; cry aloud, and spare not; lift up your voice like a trumpet, and tell the people the error of their doings. I shall ever love the thought of a woman preaching the gospel. I myself went to hear one out of curiosity, and God made it his opportunity to bless me with his grace, nineteen years ago. . . . May you devote body, and soul, and spirit to his glory, and never tire till death your soul remove.[8]

Next to her future husband, Zechariah Taft, Mary had no more enthusiastic supporter than William Bramwell. "The design of God concerning you," he reminded her, "is to spread the flame of heavenly love in our connexion." He went on to say that if she thought her work was done—obsolete—"I think differently. A number of places will yet receive you; and I think your way is more open this Conference than ever it has been."[9] Michael Fenwick's esteem for her was no less grand. "God himself has sent you," he admonished her, "like the great Wesley, and the great Whitfield; namely, as a blessing to the nation."[10]

Mary's passionate desire to save souls cut across the increasing respectability of the Methodist Societies. She defied their conservatism. Her revivalistic spirit created anxiety among some of the faithful members of established chapels. Her opponents criticized the emotionalism that often swept through her spellbound congregations. Some of her critics stooped so low as to spread slanderous rumors concerning her. "She is a man," some claimed, "in woman's clothes." "She had abandoned her children," others gossiped, "and left her family to fen for themselves." The mudslinging was fierce at times and a perennial source of anguish to Mary.

Tensions were rising. One letter from the period reveals something of the clash between spirited revivalism and measured respectability:

> We have had a Miss Mary Barritt in this circuit. . . . She has been made very useful in the hands of God at many places; indeed at Darlington, they attribute the great revival there chiefly to her instrumentality; and I believe, there might have been many more saved here, had not some of us been too prejudiced to suffer a woman to preach in public—too orderly to detain the people at the prayer-meetings, past such a time of night.[11]

After Wesley's death, in that amazing dynamic of structure and spirit, institutional survival was beginning to take precedence over the unpredictability of grace. The women preachers found themselves caught right in the middle. The stage was set for an explosive confrontation.

## On Pain of Excommunication

In the summer of 1802, Joseph Entwisle wrote to his colleague Jonathan Edmondson concerning the situation in his new circuit at Macclesfield:

> We have no female preachers in this part of the country. I think women might with propriety exercise their gifts in a private way, or amongst their own sex; but I never could see the propriety of their being public teachers. Under the Patriarchal dispensation, the oldest male was the priest of the family. Under the Law, all the priests were men. The seventy preachers sent out by our Lord were all men. So were the twelve Apostles. Nor do we ever read of a woman preaching, in the Acts of the Apostles. Hence I conclude, women are not designed for public teachers.[12]

As Methodism entered the nineteenth century, this conservative, restrictive attitude became increasingly dominant. A radical form of regression took place in this new era.

At the Dublin Conference for Irish Methodism, in July 1802, a serious debate took place over the question of women's preaching. Even public exhortation was vehemently opposed. Hostility toward the female preachers rose to fever pitch. In spite of the overwhelming success of women such as Alice Cambridge and Anne Brown, their male counterparts took extreme and immediate action to repress their activities: "It is the judgment of the Conference, that it is contrary both to Scripture and prudence that women should preach, or should exhort in public: and we direct the Superintendent to refuse a Society Ticket to any woman in the Methodist Connexion who preaches, or who exhorts in any public congregation, unless she entirely cease from so doing."[13]

By this action, Alice Cambridge was immediately excluded from the Society. She was prohibited from using any Methodist chapel or property for her evangelistic services. By way of a letter, on July 29, 1802, Zechariah Taft informed his colleague, Mary Barritt, of the momentous developments: "I was thankful to hear of your success in Grimsby Circuit—what would the Irish Brethren say to this—they have passed an act in their conference held the 2 of this month that no Woman should preach or exhort in public upon pain of Excommunication."[14] It took a special resolution of the Irish Conference of 1811 to restore Alice's status as a member of the Methodist Society. Her success was just too overwhelming to ignore or deny. After 1813 she devoted herself entirely to a ministry of evangelism that attracted enormous crowds in the north of Ireland.

After Mary Barritt's marriage to the foremost advocate of women preachers, Zechariah Taft, on August 17, 1802, she traveled with her husband to Canterbury and on to his new appointment at Dover. Taking the bull by the horns,

she preached her first sermon there on the text: "Suffer me
that I may speak; and after that I have spoken, mock on."
Invitations to preach inundated this gifted couple. On
October 7, 1802, the *Kentish Herald* published a favorable
report concerning Mary and her work in the cathedral city
of Canterbury:

> On Monday evening, a sermon was preached in King-
> Street chapel, in this city, by Mrs. Taft, a female preacher, in
> the connexion of the late Rev. John Wesley. The novelty of
> a female preacher naturally excited great curiosity; many
> hundreds of persons were present, and others were pre-
> vented from getting in for want of room. The text of her
> discourse was from the first epistle of St. John, the first
> chapter, and the ninth verse—"If we confess our sins, he is
> faithful and just to forgive us our sins, and to cleanse us
> from all unrighteousness;" which she supported with many
> judicious and well-grounded remarks; and being possessed
> with great fluency of speech, she attracted great attention
> from the whole of the congregation.[15]

Joseph Benson was incensed. He fired off a caustic letter
to Mary's husband expressing his outrage. The Conference, he claimed sarcastically, was ignorant about Taft's
"taking a female to assist him in the ministry." Then he
added: "What the District Meeting or the Conference may
say to you for deceiving them in this manner, I am not certain. . . . Mrs. Taft should decline ascending the pulpits of
the chapels unless Mr. Sykes, Mr. Rogers, and you be less
sufficient for your work than the Conference supposed you
to be."[16]

George Sykes, who was the newly appointed Superintendent, countered Benson's diatribe with a strong letter of
defense:

> We find two Mary Apostlesses to the Apostles. I have
> had a personal acquaintance with Mary Barritt for more
> than eight years. I dare not oppose her. . . . More than a
> year and a half ago, Mary Barritt was strongly pressed by
> our Hull friends to visit them; the elders of the Society sat

in counsel. . . . The conclusion was not to admit her into the pulpit, but allow her to stand by the little desk in the chapel. But after once hearing this ram's horn, prejudices fell down like the walls of Jericho, the pulpit door gave way, and this King's daughter entered, the chapel could not contain the people, hundreds stood in the street. She then preached abroad to thousands, and solemn reverence sat on their countenances to the very skirts of the huge assembly.[17]

John Pawson wrote to the Society at Dover, expressing his pleasure at the providence that stationed Mary among them. In this important letter, which helped to pave the way for her ministry in that circuit, Pawson explains how "the Lord is pleased to go out of his common way sometimes for the good of his poor creatures." "I have been no great friend to women preaching among us," he continues, "but when I evidently see that good is done, I dare not forbid them." Fully aware of the controversy that was beginning to arise, he concludes: "I would therefore advise you by no means oppose her preaching, but let her have full liberty, and try whether the Lord will not make her an instrument of reviving his work among you."[18]

Pawson wrote to the Tafts once again at the beginning of the new year. He expressed his regret concerning the storm that had arisen in Kent at the outset of their ministry together. Having weathered the initial blast, however, he encouraged them both to press on in hopes of spiritual renewal and growth in that place. He rejoiced over the fact that his intervention proved helpful in reconciling many to her ministry:

I am very glad that those good men at Dover were not offended with my letter, and much more so to find that the door was now opened wide for the partner of your life, to use the gifts which the Lord hath given her, for the enlargement of his kingdom. He will send by whom he will send, and it does not become us to say to the infinitely wise and blessed God,—"What doest thou?" but rather to rejoice when we have reason to believe that he doth good by the instrumentality of any one. An apostle could rejoice, even when Christ was preached out of envy and strife. I have long been convinced that the Lord takes such methods, and uses such instruments in reviving, increasing, and carrying on his work, as hath a direct tendency to hide pride from man, and so convince every one that this is the work of God,—so that no flesh may glory in his sight, but that he who glorieth, may glory in the Lord.[19]

The extremely vocal critics of women's preaching were not willing to let the matter rest. Controversy erupted once again when the preachers gathered at Manchester for the Conference of 1803. A question was posed: "Should women be permitted to preach among the Methodists?" And the following restrictive resolution was passed, not without some pressure from the hierarchy:

We are of the opinion that, in general, they ought not. 1. Because a vast majority of our people are opposed to it. 2. Because their preaching does not at all seem necessary, there being a sufficiency of Preachers, whom God has accredited, to supply all the places in our connexion with regular preaching. But if any woman among us think she has an extraordinary call from God to speak in public, (and we are sure it must be an *extraordinary* call that can authorize it,) we are of opinion she should, in general, address her *own sex* and *those only*. And, upon this condition alone, should any woman be permitted to preach in any part of our connexion; and, when so permitted, it should be under the following regulations: 1. They shall not preach in the Circuit where they reside, until they have obtained the approbation of the Superintendent and a Quarterly Meeting. 2. Before they go into any other Circuit to preach, they shall have a *written* invitation from the Superintendent from such Circuit, and a recommendatory note from the Superintendent of their own Circuit.[20]

The women preachers hereby received the formal censure of the Wesleyan Methodist leaders. The die was cast for at least a century to follow. These restrictions severely impeded the influence that the women could exert over the hardening institution. After 1803, many of the aspiring women preachers found it necessary to leave their Methodist home in order to fulfill their Christian vocation. Some found sanction for their activities within the larger pale of the Methodist tradition, becoming associated with the new Wesleyan groups of the early nineteenth century. At the originating Conference of the Bible Christians, for instance, in 1819, fourteen of the itinerant preachers were women. Similar numbers flocked to the Primitive Methodists.

The restrictive resolution of the Conference remained in effect until it was revised in 1910. The only change at that time, however, was the deletion of the words restricting the preaching of women to their own sex. And a proviso was added restricting their activities to areas where there was little or no opposition to their work. This then was the official position within Wesleyan Methodism until the Methodist union of 1932. Matters concerning women preachers arose from time to time. For instance, in 1832 a large amount of discussion was devoted to the work of the so-called "Derby Faith Folk" and the Arminian Methodists. Elizabeth Evans was their shining light, George Eliot's model for the fascinating character of Dinah Morris in her novel *Adam Bede*. But no formal actions were ever taken by the Conference.

In spite of the severe shortage of itinerant preachers at the time of the 1804 Conference, the leadership was resolute in its stand against the women. William Bramwell, one of Mary Taft's most ardent supporters, bemoaned the decisive action of his ministerial colleagues: "That rule should not have been submitted to. This I advised, and had all the friends stood firm, it would never have been made. But as it is made, and complied with, I would advise you to act according to it in every thing, whilst in the connexion. This is right,—whilst in the Body, to submit to all rules made by that Body."[21] Mary Taft did submit. She meticulously conformed to the regulations established by the Conference, and continued to preach. But she was an exception. For all intents and purposes, the voices of the women within the Wesleyan Methodist Church were silenced. They would find their voice anew, however, in a future wave of dramatic social change. In the ebb and flow of social and religious currents, they would find themselves, once again, on the crest of the wave.

# Epilogue

## The Legacy

The journey of the women preachers of early Methodism was long and arduous. A saga of pain and perseverance lies hidden within the fragments of their lost history. Unquestionably, the women preachers helped to make the evangelical revival of the eighteenth century a powerful religious movement of enduring significance. Women were conspicuous as pioneers in the establishment and expansion of Methodism. The women preachers proclaimed a message of hope and liberation to the world of their day. Their lives were a living testimony to the power of life lived unto God, of faith working by love. Acceptance of their calling as preachers, however, involved a painful process of real transformation.

An important question emerges out of these facts that is not without significance in our own time. Why is it that women tend to find enlarged opportunity for witness and service in the renewal movements of Christianity? A corollary question is, perhaps, of even greater significance. What is it about the process of institutionalization that tends to push women to the fringe of the structures? One perennial task of the church is to maintain a dynamic balance between the spirit and the structures. The "woman question" always plays a crucial part in that dynamic tension.

We also live in a time of great renewal within the life of the Christian community. God's call upon the lives of women today is real. Women who are called to preach continue to struggle with the failure of many to accept their vocation in life. The question of women preachers has become, once again, an issue of critical debate within the Christian family. In Methodism, as we have seen, a wealth of factors combined to create a climate conducive to the acceptance and empowerment of women preachers. Three factors seem to have been particularly significant: Wesley's understanding of the place and role of women and women preachers in particular, the theological dynamic of the Wesleyan movement, and the supportive environment of the Methodist Society.

The status of the women preachers within the Wesleyan revival cannot be understood apart from the person of John Wesley. Much of his appreciation for the place of his female colleagues in the life of the church can be traced to his formative years in the Epworth rectory. His attitudes and actions changed dramatically over the course of several decades. But, largely due to the influence of his mother, Susanna, Wesley seldom wavered from this fundamental principle: No one, including a woman, ought to be prohibited from doing God's work in obedience to the inner calling of her conscience. It was this conviction that led him, not only to sanction but also to encourage the controversial practice of women's preaching in his day.

Second, the egalitarian impulse of the Wesleyan revival was founded upon certain principles held in common with most renewal movements. Among these primary tenets are the value of individual persons, the possibility of direct communion with God, the emphasis on the present activity of the Holy Spirit in the life of the believer, the importance placed upon shared Christian experience, the rights of conscience, and the doctrine of the priesthood of all believers. These views all combined to create a theological atmosphere conducive to the empowerment of women.

Wesley's goal was personal religious experience and its power to transform both individuals and society. His dynamic view of salvation and the Christian life transcended sexual and social distinctions. Christian vocation is a gift of grace offered to all. The unity and equality of all believers in Christ (Gal. 3:28) became an inherent aspect of the evangelical preaching of Wesleyan itinerants. Not only was faith to be expressed in the works of all, but individual talents were also to be developed as a sacred trust from God. These attitudes undercut prevailing stereotypes about the status and role of women in society. The preaching of women was a natural progression, a logical extension of the Wesleyan theology of religious experience.

Third, the Methodist Society provided a liberating environment for women. The early pioneers who were responsible for the initiation of new Societies naturally assumed positions of leadership. By allowing women to assume important positions of leadership within the structure of the Societies, Wesley gave concrete expression to the freedom he proclaimed in his preaching. Individuals who stood on the periphery of English society were empowered and gifted for service. Women progressed through the ranks of the Methodist Societies in response to God's claim on their lives. Their gifts were acknowledged. Mutual accountability and encouragement enhanced their sense of self-esteem and purpose. They were empowered by their ability to give.

As band and class leaders, visitors of the sick, and exhorters within the Societies, many women functioned, for all intents and purposes, as sub-pastors. They felt free to express themselves and to exercise their gifts. They led the Methodist family in their simple acts of worship and service. The Methodist Society, therefore, provided an invaluable support system for women who felt called by God into activities traditionally reserved for men. In the rich soil of the Methodist Society, the women preachers were nurtured, allowed to mature both in gifts and graces, and affirmed in the harvesting of abundant fruit.

The stories of the women preachers are compelling. Their faith is contagious. Their robust message of a full, free, and present salvation is a gospel we need to reclaim. As we draw this study to a close, there could be no more fitting tribute to the women preachers of early Methodism and their legacy than to let one of these pioneers proclaim her message of God's love in Christ in her own words.

The excerpts that follow are unique since they come from the only extant sermon of a pioneer in the first generation of Methodist women preachers. In this powerful exposition of Acts 27:29, Mary Fletcher describes the "creating and redeeming love of God" and the "promises" of God in Christ. These are the anchors of a living faith. These are the sources of hope and life that sustained the women in their arduous pilgrimage of faithful discipleship.

> Let us try to cast out one anchor now. I am sensible your cable is short, therefore we must seek for some ground as *near* you as we can. We will try, if we can, to find it in the *creating love of God*, surrounding us on every side. Look through the creation—observe the tender love of the birds toward their young, yea, even the most savage beasts! From whence does this spring? It is from God. It is a shadow of that infinite compassion which reigns in his heart.
>
> Rise a little higher. Fix your eye on man. How does he love a stubborn son who will neither serve God nor him? . . . If that son shed but a tear of sorrow—raise but a sigh of repentance—if he but come a few steps, . . . how doth [the father] run to meet him!
>
> Believe, then, that this "Author of all love is more ready to give the Holy Spirit to you, than you are to give good gifts to your children." Will not this anchor take? Does it still come home? Well, the ground is good, but your cable is too short. Let us try another anchor; and we will drop it on *Redeeming love*.
>
> Lift up your eyes of faith—behold your bleeding Saviour! See all your sins laid on his sacred head! . . . He hath

drunk all the bitter cup for *you,* and he offers this night to take you into fellowship and communion with himself. . . . Come, let me hear some voice among you giving praise, and saying with the Christian poet:

> Now I have found the ground wherein
> *Sure* my soul's anchor may remain;
> he wounds of Jesus for my sin,
> Before the world's foundation slain.

But perhaps there are some poor trembling souls still left behind. For the sake of such, we will try to find firm ground a little nearer yet. We will drop our third anchor on the *Promises.* Here are some quite within your reach, "He that cometh unto me, I will in no wise cast out. Whosoever will, let him take of the water of life freely. I came not to call the righteous, but sinners to repentance." Yes, "He came to seek and to save that which is lost." Are *you* lost? Lost in your own estimation? Then he came to *save you.* Yes, and to *seek* you too, and he seeks you this night as diligently as ever shepherd sought his lost sheep.

Here is the great design of the wonderful plan of salvation—to restore man to his original communion with God; and he who hath said, "I will give unto him that is athirst of the water of life freely"—now waits to make your souls his loved abode, the temple of indwelling God. There is a rest which remains for the people of God; and you who love the Lord, remember, "He came not only that you might have life," but that "you may have it more abundantly." . . . For the very end of our creation is, that we may become "the habitation of God through the Spirit."[1]

This was the message of the early Methodist women preachers. The core of their good news was a profound optimism in God's grace linked with holiness of heart and life. And the present experience of God's love, they believed, was both personally transforming and socially redeeming. The women preachers offered the fullness of God's grace in Christ for all. And their urgent message is as compelling today as ever!

O that you would do as Jacob did, be earnest with the Lord, that his love may fill your heart, as the Scripture expresses it, the love of God, shed abroad in your hearts by the Holy Ghost, given unto you.[2]

Women, having been awakened by the proclamation of God's love for them as unique human beings, experienced adoption as the children of God. They asserted their claim as co-heirs with Christ. Each woman brought her own gifts to the Lord of Love and offered them up for the building of God's new age. To the lost she offered signposts for the pilgrim journey. To the least she proclaimed a message of hope. To the last she described a new order in God's love that is characterized by a radical reversal of place. She offered them Christ. Her legacy must never be forgotten! Philippians 4:3

# For Further Reading

This brief bibliographical appendix is meant to be a guide to further reading in the broad area of Christian women's studies. While the focus of this book has been on the Methodist tradition, it is hoped that the legacy you have encountered has opened wider vistas to your view. I have intentionally restricted this survey to material that is relatively easy to locate or acquire. Many of these works contain bibliographical aids that can lead you into further study or inspiring reading.

The best starting point for an exploration of the roles of women in the life of the church is Christian biography. Edith Deem's *Great Women of the Christian Faith* (New York: Harper, 1959) was an early attempt to compile biographical sketches of outstanding women and is still generally reliable. A more recent parallel volume is Nancy A. Hardesty's *Great Women of Faith* (Nashville: Abingdon, 1980). One attractive feature of this collection is Hardesty's focus upon the consistency of word and deed in the lives of the women reviewed. The three-volume work of the late, distinguished church historian Roland Bainton, entitled *Women of the Reformation* (Minneapolis: Augsburg, 1971–1977), must also be included among these collections of vignettes.

The feminist movement, however, has engendered an

explosion of research that seeks to revise our understanding of the past, not simply to compensate for neglect in previous ages. Not only have scholars added formerly invisible women into the general portrait, but in the process have also found it necessary to completely reconstruct our image of the past. Elisabeth Schüssler Fiorenza's *In Memory of Her: A Feminist Theological Reconstruction of Christian Origins* (New York: Crossroad, 1983) stands out as a model for this process. *Women of Spirit: Female Leadership in the Jewish and Christian Traditions* (New York: Simon & Schuster, 1979), edited by Ruether and McLaughlin, charts similar territory in an effort to recover lost chapters of history and to create new paradigms of understanding. Another important work, *The Underside of History: A View of Women Through Time* (Boulder, Colo.: Westview, 1976), by Elise Boulding is a systematic attempt to reconstruct history, as the title implies, from the perspective of oppressed women.

In 1980, Kenneth E. Rowe prepared a bibliographical pamphlet for The United Methodist Church's General Commission on Archives and History entitled *Methodist Women: A Guide to the Literature* (World Methodist Council, Lake Junaluska, North Carolina). This is an invaluable aid for locating resources specifically related to this tradition. A two-volume set entitled *Women in New Worlds* (Nashville: Abingdon, 1981, 1982), edited by Thomas and Keller; and Keller, Queen, and Thomas respectively, is a unique collection of essays providing historical perspectives on women in the Wesleyan tradition. The rich and varied stories presented in these volumes provide an unparalleled portrait of women in Methodism. Somewhat less accessible, and considerably more expensive, is Kent Brown's *Women in Mr. Wesley's Methodism* (Mellon), which focuses upon the roles of women in early Methodism.

When we turn to the question of Methodist women preachers, resources are virtually inaccessible. Most of the primary and secondary works referred to in the text of this book may be found either in theological libraries or specialist research facilities. This is unfortunate, for there is a wealth of interesting and relevant information to be culled from the pages of numerous diaries, journals, letters, and biographies. The biographies of many of these women, based upon these resources, are yet to be written.

The one exception to this general rule is material related to Susanna Wesley, who has been revered more as a mother than as a person of tremendous stature in her own right. The most thoroughly documented study of Susanna is John A. Newton's *Susanna Wesley and the Puritan Tradition in Methodism* (London: Epworth, 1968). This volume may be supplemented by the outstanding popular biography by Rebecca Harmon, *Susanna, Mother of the Wesleys* (Nashville: Abingdon, 1968). Together, these books afford a rich portrait of this greatly neglected figure. For those who have ready access to a theological library, John Newton provides a judicious summary of biographical material in "Susanna Wesley (1669–1742): A Bibliographical Survey" (*Wesley Historical Society, Proceedings*, 37 [June 1969]: 37-41).

With regard to the contemporary debate concerning the status and role of women in the church, I will only mention several titles out of a rapidly expanding body of literature. One little pamphlet that remains a classic is Krister Stendahl's *The Bible and the Role of Women* (Minneapolis: Fortress, 1966). Stendahl affords a cogently argued biblical view of male and female in which both emancipation and ordination may be embraced. Two ecumenical studies on the ordination of women are of value. In her *When the Minister Is a Woman* (Troy, Mo.: Holt, Rinehart & Winston, 1970), Elsie Gibson draws on a number of surveys and studies to show that sexual inequities often remain in church structures regardless of ordination. And a more recent study, entitled *Ordination of Women in Ecumenical Perspective* (World Council of Churches, 1980), edited by Constance F. Parvey, provides an up-to-date examination of the status of women clergy across the spectrum of the church. A simple, readable, and more practical guide to the leadership of women in the church is *Women as Pastors* (Nashville: Abingdon, 1982), in the Creative Leadership Series edited by Lyle E. Schaller.

For those among you who prefer a good novel to the path of scholarly pursuits, I cannot fail to mention the George Eliot classic, *Adam Bede,* the central character of which, Dinah Morris, was based upon one of the most noted female preachers of the early nineteenth century, Elizabeth Evans.

In all of your pursuits in this area, be they academic or inspiration, my prayer is that something of these women's devotion to Christ and their compassion for others will have a transforming effect on your lives. In the rediscovery and sharing of their lives, we are all blessed.

# Notes

## 1. A Process of Liberation Begins

1. John Robinson, *The Works of John Robinson*, ed. Robert Ashton, 3 vols. (London: John Snow, 1851) 3:55.
2. Arthur Lake, *Sermons with some religious and divine meditations*, 3 vols. (London: Printed by W. Stansby for N. Butler, 1629) 3:78 (spellings modernized). The woman preacher in question may have been Dorothy (Kelly) Hazard, a famous preacher of the Broadmead (Baptist) Chapel in Bristol.
3. John Vickers, *The Schismatick Sifted*, quoted in Julia O'Faolain and Laurel Martines, eds., *Not in God's Image: Women in History from the Greeks to the Victorians* (New York: Harper & Row, 1973), p. 264.
4. John Rogers, *Ohel or Beth-shemesh* (London: R. I. and G. and H. Eversden, 1653), II. viii.
5. Herbert Butterfield, "England in the Eighteenth Century," in *A History of the Methodist Church in Great Britain*, ed. Rupert Davies and Gordon Rupp, 4 vols. (London: Epworth Press, 1965– ) 1:23-24.
6. *The Gentlemen's Magazine: Or, Monthly Intelligencer* 5, 9 (September 1735): 555.
7. John Wesley, *The Journal of the Rev. John Wesley, A. M.*, ed. Nehemiah Curnock, 8 vols. (London: Epworth Press, 1909–1916) 3:32.
8. Susanna Wesley to Lady Yarborough, March 7, 1702, quoted in Robert Walmsley, "John Wesley's Parents: Quarrel and Reconciliation," *Wesley Historical Society, Proceedings*, 29, 3 (September 1953): 52.
9. Susanna Wesley to Samuel Wesley, February 6, 1712, as quoted in Wesley, *Journal*, 3:32.
10. John Whitehead, *The Life of the Rev. John Wesley, A. M.*, 2 vols. (London: Couchman, 1793, 1796), 1:47-48.
11. Ibid., p. 54.

12. V. H. H. Green, *The Young Mr. Wesley: A Study of John Wesley and Oxford* (London: Arnold, 1961), pp. 53-54.
13. The reflections of Alexander Knox, as printed in Robert Southey, *The Life of Wesley: and the Rise and Progress of Methodism*, new ed., 2 vols. (London: Longman, Green, Roberts & Green, 1864), 2:295.
14. Margaret Bovey (afterwards Mrs. James Burnside), Mrs. Robert Gilbert, and Mrs. Mary Vanderplank all served as deaconesses under Wesley's direction. See Wesley, *Journal*, 1:239-46, 272, 276, 314, 329, 337, 364-69, 376, 387.
15. John Wesley to Mrs. Fox, November 24, 1738, in John Wesley, *The Works of John Wesley*, ed. Frank Baker (Oxford: Clarendon Press, 1980, 1982), 25:588-89.
16. John Wesley to J. Hutton and Mr. Fox, November 24, 1738, in Wesley, *Works* (Oxford ed.), 25:588.

## 2. On the Cutting Edge of Revival

1. James Lackington, *Memoirs*, new ed. (London: By the Author, 1794), p. 123.
2. John Wesley, *The Journal of the Rev. John Wesley, A. M.*, ed. Nehemiah Curnock, 8 vols. (London: Epworth Press, 1909–1916) 2:174.
3. July 23, 1740, ibid., 2:371.
4. Thomas Jackson, ed., *The Lives of the Early Methodist Preachers*, 4th ed., 6 vols. (London: Wesleyan Conference Office, 1875), 1:60.
5. Abraham Watmough, *A History of Methodism in the City of Lincoln* (Lincoln: Printed by R. E. Leary, 1829), p. 24. This letter of January 18, 1788, apparently escaped the attention of Telford in his standard edition of Wesley's letters.
6. Wesley, *Journal*, 3:103.
7. William Bowman, *The Imposture of Methodism Display'd* (London: Printed for Joseph Lord, 1740), p. 27.
8. Charles Wesley, *The Journal of the Rev. Charles Wesley, M.A.*, ed. Thomas Jackson, 2 vols. (London: John Mason, 1849), 1:152.
9. Charles Wesley, *Journal*, 1:307. His allusion to the Pauline prohibitions is evident.
10. John Wesley, *The Letters of the Rev. John Wesley, A. M.*, ed. John Telford, 8 vols. (London: Epworth Press, 1931), 2:119-20. This publication, "A Letter to a Person lately join'd with the People call'd Quakers," passed through no less than three editions that same year. It was subsequently reprinted in Wesley's famous *Preservations against Unsettled Notions in Religion*.
11. George Lavington, *The Enthusiasm of Methodists and Papists Compar'd, Part II* (London: J. and P. Knapton, 1749), p. 126.
12. Wesley, *Works* (Oxford ed.), 11:406.

## 3. She Led the Way to Zion

1. John Wesley, *The Letters of the Rev. John Wesley, A.M.*, ed. John Telford, 8 vols. (London: Epworth Press, 1931), 6:233.

2. Joseph Sutcliffe, *The Experience of Mrs. Frances Pawson* (London: Printed at the Conference Office, by Thomas Cordeux, 1813), p. 84.

3. John Wesley, *The Works of the Rev. John Wesley, A.M.*, ed. Thomas Jackson, 14 vols. (London: Mason, 1829–31), 8:263.

4. Sermon XCVIII. "On Visiting the Sick," in ibid., 7:125-26.

5. William Bennet, *Memoirs of Mrs. Grace Bennet* (Macclesfield: E. Bayley, 1803), p. 29.

6. Ibid., pp. 13-14.

7. Ibid., p. 19.

8. William W. Stamp, *The Orphan-House of Wesley: Early Methodism in Newcastle-upon-Tyne* (London: John Mason, 1863), p. 48.

9. Wesley's manuscript account is preserved in the British Library and has been accurately reproduced in J. Augustin Leger, *John Wesley's Last Love* (London: J. M. Dent & Sons, 1910).

10. John Wesley to Charles Wesley, June 23, 1739, in John Wesley, *The Works of John Wesley*, ed. Frank Baker (Oxford: Clarendon Press, 1980, 1982), 25:660.

11. Ibid., 26:206.

12. Ibid., pp. 610-11.

13. See Frank Baker, *John Wesley and the Church of England* (Nashville: Abingdon Press, 1970), p. 83.

14. *A Review of the Policy, Doctrines and Morals of the Methodists* (London: J. Johnson, 1791), p. 8.

### 4. Did She Preach, or Not?

1. John Pipe, "Memoir of Miss Isabella Wilson," *Methodist Magazine* 31 (1808): 461.

2. John Wesley, *The Journal of the Rev. John Wesley, A.M.*, ed. Nehemiah Curnock, 8 vols. (London: Epworth Press, 1909–1916) 5:94.

3. William Bramwell, *A Short Account of the Life and Death of Ann Cutler* (York: Printed by John Will, 1827), p. 6.

4. "Some Account of Sarah Peters," *Arminian Magazine* 5 (1782): 128.

5. Ibid., p. 129.

6. Wesley, *Journal*, 3:250.

7. Ibid., 6:126.

8. Ibid., 4:471.

9. Ibid., p. 432.

10. Ibid., 5:371.

11. Sarah Crosby, MS Letterbook, 1760–1774, Perkins Library, Duke University, pp. 111-13.

12. John Wesley to Jane Hilton, in John Wesley, *The Letters of the Rev. John Wesley, A.M.*, ed. John Telford, 8 vols. (London: Epworth Press, 1931), 5:128.

13. John Wesley to Jane Barton, in ibid., p. 151.

14. Bramwell, *Life and Death of Ann Cutler*, p. 21.

15. Wesley, *Letters*, 6:94.

16. Ibid., 4:202.
17. *A Short Account of Mrs. Elizabeth Maxfield* (London: Printed by J. W. Pasham, 1778), p. 30.
18. Zechariah Taft, *Biographical Sketches of Holy Women*, 2 vols. (London: Kershaw, 1825; Leeds: Cullingworth and J. Stephens, 1828), 1:128.
19. Ibid., p. 97.
20. Ibid., p. 201.
21. Wesley, *Letters*, 4:51-52.
22. "Ought We to Separate from the Church of England?" as quoted in Frank Baker, *John Wesley and the Church of England* (Nashville: Abingdon Press, 1970), p. 333. This same view is expressed in his later sermon, "The Ministerial Office."

### 5. Experimenting With or Without a Pulpit

1. "The Grace of God Manifested, In an Account of Mrs. Crosby, of Leeds," *Arminian Magazine* 29 (1806): 420-21
2. Henry Moore, *The Life of Mrs. Mary Fletcher*, 6th ed. (London: J. Kershaw, 1824), p. 27.
3. *Arminian Magazine* 29:466-67.
4. Ibid., p. 470.
5. Ibid., p. 518. Notice the similarities between this account and the experience of Susanna Wesley in the Epworth rectory.
6. Ibid.
7. John Wesley, *The Letters of the Rev. John Wesley, A.M.*, ed. John Telford, 8 vols. (London: Epworth Press, 1931), 4:133.
8. *Arminian Magazine*, 29:164.
9. The letter clearly lacks a strip down the left margin of the first page. Telford attempted to reconstruct the letter with only partial success. See Wesley, *Letters*, 4:164. For a full discussion of the letter and evidence concerning its reconstruction, see Paul W. Chilcote, "John Wesley and the Women Preachers of Early Methodism" (Ph.D. diss., Duke University, 1984), pp. 355-56.
10. John Wesley, *Explanatory Notes upon the New Testament* (London: Bowyer, 1755), 1 Corinthians 14:34.
11. Sarah Crosby to Mr. Oddie, at the New Room, in the Horse Fair, Bristol, from London, January 28, 1763, Methodist Archives, Rylands Library, University of Manchester.
12. Moore, *Life of Mrs. Mary Fletcher*, p. 29.
13. January 4, 1758, John Wesley, *The Journal of the Rev. John Wesley, A.M.*, ed. Nehemiah Curnock, 8 vols. (London: Epworth Press, 1909–1916) 4:247.
14. Ibid., 5:102. Wesley founded the Kingswood School near Bristol upon the model of Francke's Orphan School in Halle.
15. Moore, *Life of Mrs. Mary Fletcher*, pp. 46-47.
16. *Minutes of the Methodist Conferences* (London: Conference Office), 1:52.
17. Sarah Crosby to Mrs. ——, July 7, 1765, MS Letterbook, pp. 37-38.

18. Wesley, *Journal*, 5:195.
19. Wesley, *Letters*, 5:46.
20. Moore, *Life of Mrs. Mary Fletcher*, p. 77.
21. Wesley, *Letters*, 5:130.
22. Ibid., p. 113.
23. "Account of Mrs. Hannah Harrison," *Methodist Magazine* 25 (1802): 318.
24. Wesley, *Letters*, 5:150.
25. Ibid., p. 193.
26. Ibid., p. 157.

## 6. Extraordinary Women for Extraordinary Tasks

1. The text is based upon the first publication of the letter in Zechariah Taft, *The Scripture Doctrine of Women's Preaching: Stated and Examined* (York: R. and J. Richardson, 1820), pp. 19-20. It has been compared with the manuscript copy of the letter in Crosby, MS Letterbook, pp. 55-61. No major textual variations were noted.
2. From the manuscript in Methodist Archives, correcting Wesley, in John Wesley, *The Letters of the Rev. John Wesley, A.M.*, ed. John Telford, 8 vols. (London: Epworth Press, 1931), 5:257.
3. Ibid., pp. 257-58.
4. Ibid., 6:290-91.
5. Rufus M. Jones, *The Later Periods of Quakerism*, 2 vols. (London: Macmillan, 1921), 1:198.
6. Wesley, *Letters*, 7:8-9.
7. "The Experience of Mrs. Ann Gilbert, of Gwinear, in Cornwall," *Arminian Magazine* 18 (1795): 44.
8. Zechariah Taft, *Biographical Sketches of Holy Women*, 2 vols. (London: Kershaw, 1825; Leeds: Cullingworth and J. Stephens, 1828), 1:50-51.
9. Ibid., p. 51.
10. Quoted in C. H. Crookshank, *History of Methodism in Ireland*, 3 vols. (Belfast: R. S. Allen, 1885), 1:182. See John Wesley, *The Journal of the Rev. John Wesley, A.M.*, ed. Nehemiah Curnock, 8 vols. (London: Epworth Press, 1909–1916) 5:113.
11. Edward Smyth, ed., *The Extraordinary Life and Christian Experience of Margaret Davidson, As Dictated by Herself* (Dublin: Dugdale, 1782), p. 97.
12. Taft, *Holy Women*, 1:178-79.
13. Ibid., p. 181.
14. The text is the transcript of a letter/draft in the handwriting of the Reverend Joseph Benson, Number 167 in the W. L. Watkinson Collection, New Room, Bristol. The manuscript contains no postal markings of any kind and is most certainly a draft of a letter sent to a Methodist itinerant preacher. It may be assigned a provisional date of October 1775.
15. April 1, 1773, Dublin, Wesley, *Letters*, 6:23.

16. December 26, 1776, London, ibid., pp. 245-46.
17. Ibid., p. 23.
18. Mary frequently preached from Old Testament passages, this reference to Daniel 3:16 being the first recorded text in her journal as quoted in Henry Moore, *The Life of Mrs. Mary Fletcher,* 6th ed. (London: J. Kershaw, 1824), p. 98.
19. *Arminian Magazine* 29:295.
20. Moore, *Life of Mrs. Mary Fletcher,* p. 103.
21. May 28, 1775, ibid., p. 107.
22. Ibid., pp. 107-8.
23. Ibid., pp. 117-19.
24. Ibid., p. 120.
25. Taft, *Holy Women,* 2:69.
26. Ibid., 1:104. See also Isabella Mackiver's interesting account of Sarah's visits in Scarborough in Susan C. Brooke, "The Journal of Isabella Mackiver," *Wesley Historical Society, Proceedings* 28, 8 (December 1952): 161.
27. Taft, *Holy Women,* 2:84.
28. *Arminian Magazine* 29:567.
29. Joseph Sutcliffe, *The Experience of Mrs. Frances Pawson* (London: T. Cordeux, 1813), p. 33.
30. Sarah Crosby to Elizabeth Hurrell, Cross Hall, July 2, 1774, Crosby, MS Letterbrook, pp. 69-71.
31. Taft, *Holy Women,* 2:75.
32. Luke Tyerman, *Wesley's Designated Successor: The Life, Letters, and Literary Labours of the Rev. John William Fletcher, Vicar of Madeley, Shropshire* (London: Hodder and Stoughton, 1882), pp. 400-401. Fletcher was later to become the husband of Mary Bosanquet. This is one of the very few explicit statements that he made on the question of women preachers, although he was one of their strong advocates. The obvious biblical allusion is to Acts 2:28, in which the prophet Joel is quoted.

## 7. "Female Brethren" Among the Men

1. Richard Collett, unpublished manuscript account of the life of Elizabeth Tonkin Collett.
2. Zechariah Taft, *Biographical Sketches of Holy Women,* 2 vols. (London: Kershaw, 1825; Leeds: Cullingworth and J. Stephens, 1828), 2:116.
3. John Wesley, *The Journal of the Rev. John Wesley, A.M.,* ed. Nehemiah Curnock, 8 vols. (London: Epworth Press, 1909–1916) 6:338-39.
4. Ibid. Curnock dates this event about 1779.
5. From the journal of Adam Clarke, quoted in J. B. B. Clarke, ed., *An Account of the Life of Adam Clarke,* 3 vols. (London: T. S. Clarke, 1833) 1:215-16.
6. J. Conder Nattrass, "Some Notes from the Oldest Register of the Great Yarmouth Circuit," *Wesley Historical Society, Proceedings* 3 (1902): 74.
7. Clarke, *Life of Adam Clarke,* 1:216.

8. Taft, *Holy Women*, 2:27.
9. Wesley, *Journal*, 7:226-27. Wesley published an account of her life, written by her uncle, William Mallitt, in *Arminian Magazine* 11 (1788): 91-93, 130-33, 185-88, 238-42.
10. *Arminian Magazine* 11:92.
11. J. E. Hellier, "Some Methodist Women Preachers," *Methodist Recorder Winter Number* 36 (Christmas 1895): 66.
12. Quoted in Taft, *Holy Women*, 1:84.
13. In the early nineteenth century, Zechariah Taft possessed the original document and reproduced it in his *Holy Women*, 1:84. See John Wesley, *The Letters of the Rev. John Wesley, A.M.*, ed. John Telford, 8 vols. (London: Epworth Press, 1931), 8:15.
14. Quoted in Taft, *Holy Women*, 1:84-85.
15. Wesley, *Letters*, 8:77-78.
16. Ibid., pp. 118-19.
17. Ibid., p. 229.
18. Ibid., p. 190.
19. *Arminian Magazine* 7 (1784): 470.
20. Thomas Jackson, ed., *The Lives of the Early Methodist Preachers*, 4th ed., 6 vols. (London: Wesley Conference Office, 1875), 6:102.
21. Luke Tyerman, *Wesley's Designated Successor: The Life, Letters, and Literary Labours of the Rev. John William Fletcher, Vicar of Madeley* (London: Hodder and Stoughton, 1882), p. 502.
22. Henry Moore, *The Life of Mrs. Mary Fletcher*, 6th ed. (London: J. Kershaw, 1824), p. 154.
23. *Wesleyan Methodist Magazine* 60 (1837): 901-2.
24. Moore, *Life of Mrs. Mary Fletcher*, pp. 159-60.
25. Quoted from her journal in Hellier, "Some Methodist Women Preachers," p. 66. Wesley, who observed her preaching on numerous occasions, recorded his impression in the *Journal*. "Her words were as fire, conveying both light and heat to the hearts of all that heard her" (7:247). "[Her manner of speaking] is now smooth, easy, and natural even when the sense is deep and strong" (7:249).
26. Mary Fletcher, *An Account of Sarah Lawrence* (London: Thomas Cordeux, 1800), pp. 8-9.
27. Ibid., p. 13. Note the similarity to Susanna Wesley.
28. Ibid., p. 21.
29. J. E. Hellier, "The Mother Chapel of Leeds," *Methodist Recorder Winter Number* 35 (Christmas 1894): 64.
30. Wesley, *Letters*, 7:175-76.
31. January 31, 1791, ibid., 8:258-59.
32. June 20, 1790, Kirkstall-Forge, Zechariah Taft, *Original Letters Never Before Published, On Doctrinal, Experimental, and Practical Religion* (Whitby: George Clark, 1821), pp. 66-67. This letter was written to Mrs. Holder, who later became a preacher and assisted her itinerant husband in his circuits.

## 8. The Controversy Explodes

1. Zechariah Taft, *Original Letters Never Before Published, On Doctrinal, Experimental, and Practical Religion* (Whitby: George Clark, 1821), p. 66.
2. Quoted from her journal in Zechariah Taft, *Biographical Sketches of Holy Women,* 2 vols. (London: Kershaw, 1825; Leeds: Cullingworth and J. Stephens, 1828), 2:197.
3. Zechariah Taft, "Some Account of Elizabeth Dickinson," in William Bramwell, *A Short Account of the Life and Death of Ann Cutler* (York: Printed by John Will, 1827), p. 32.
4. Mary Taft, *Memoirs of the Life of Mrs. Mary Taft; Formerly Miss Barritt,* 2d ed., enlarged (York: M. Taft, 1828; Devon, S. Thorpe, 1831).
5. Ibid., 1:vi.
6. Ibid., p. 30.
7. Ibid., p. 64.
8. Ibid., 2:11-12. It is very probable that the woman preacher under whom he was converted was Sarah Crosby.
9. James Sigston, *A Memoir of the Life and Ministry of Mr. W. Bramwell,* 2 vols. (London: James Nichols, 1821, 1822), 1:206-7.
10. Letter of March 10, 1796, *Arminian Magazine (Bible Christian)* 3, 12 (December 1824): 431.
11. Taft, *Original Letters,* p. 103.
12. J. Entwistle, *Memoir of the Rev. Joseph Entwistle* (Bristol: J. Entwistle, 1848), p. 231.
13. *Minutes of the Methodist Conference in Ireland* (Dublin: Religious & General Book Co., 1864), p. 152. The motion was carried by a very small majority.
14. Manuscript letter in the Methodist Archives, John Rylands Library, University of Manchester.
15. Taft, *Life of Mrs. Mary Taft,* 2:49-50.
16. Joseph Benson to Z. Taft, October 2, 1802, Methodist Archives.
17. George Sykes to Joseph Benson, Methodist Archives.
18. October 25, 1802, Methodist Archives.
19. Taft, *Life of Mrs. Mary Taft,* 2:77-79.
20. *Minutes of the Methodist Conferences* (London: Conference Office, 1812– ), 2:188-89.
21. Sigston, *Life and Ministry of Mr. W. Bramwell,* 2:214-15.

## Epilogue

1. Henry Moore, *The Life of Mrs. Mary Fletcher,* 6th ed. (London: J. Kershaw, 1824), pp. 405-9.
2. Mary Tooth, *A Letter to the People of Madeley* (Shiffnal: A. Edmonds, n.d.), pp. 17-18.

# Index